DATE DUE

3·1·18			

GAYLORD   PRINTED IN U.S.A.

THE TYPEWRITER

An Illustrated History

TYPEWRITER TOPICS

With a New Introduction by
Victor M. Linoff

DOVER PUBLICATIONS, INC.
Mineola, New York

Special thanks to Wendy Inman
for her invaluable assistance in the research
and preparation of this introduction.

Bibliographical Note

This Dover edition, first published in 2000, is an unabridged reprint of *The Typewriter:
History & Encyclopedia*, first published by Typewriter Topics, New York in 1924. A new
Introduction by Victor M. Linoff has been specially prepared for this edition.

DOVER *Pictorial Archive* SERIES

International Standard Book Number: 0-486-41237-7

Manufactured in the United States of America
Dover Publications, Inc., 31 East 2nd Street, Mineola, N.Y. 11501

INTRODUCTION TO THE DOVER EDITION

The introduction of the first practical typewriter in 1873 was as significant an accomplishment in the 19th century as was Gutenberg's moveable type in the 15th century. The printing press made it possible to manufacture books and manuscripts *en masse*. In the years after its invention, much attention was given to finding a means of producing individual mechanically printed documents as an alternative to the slowness of the quill and pen, and as an improvement to the vagaries of handwriting.

Nearly 300 years would elapse before technology would permit the first primitive attempt at fashioning a mechanized substitute for the labors of handwriting. Another century would pass before the first mechanical writing device received a patent, and still another half century before a functional and reasonably reliable apparatus could be commercially manufactured and distributed.

Early contrivances were variously called the "Ktypograph," "Chirographer," "Raphigraphe," "Clavier Imprimeur," "Phonetic Writer," "Printing Machine," "Tachigraph," and "Pterotype." William A. Burt, who recorded the first U.S. patent for a mechanical writing apparatus in 1829, coined the description "Typographer." Variations of that term persisted until Christopher Latham Sholes patented the first practical writing machine as the "Type-writer" in 1868.

More than 50 men had already patented mechanical writing machines, both in the U.S. and elsewhere. But as with most complex mechanics, the one credited with an invention is most often the individual who makes the device practical. Such is the case with C.L. Sholes.

So daunting was the endeavor that Sholes enlisted additional expertise to create a workable apparatus. So it was that Carlos Glidden, a lawyer, and Samuel Soule, a civil engineer and draftsman, came to share patent credit with Sholes. It took an additional five years of improvements before a functional machine was finally offered to the public.

The initial production of 25,000, manufactured by armament maker E. Remington & Sons of Ilion, New York, was hard to sell. At about $125 each, the machines were expensive, difficult to master, awkward, and not entirely reliable. When *The Typewriter: History & Encyclopedia* was published, the public was already well acquainted with the machine; but describing this new instrument to consumers in the 1870s proved challenging. Early promotional literature touted the typewriter as "superseding the pen." It was likened in "size and appearance" to the family sewing machine; its operation

was compared to using the keys of a piano; and to a style conscious culture, it was depicted as a "graceful, ornamental and beautiful piece of furniture for any office, study or parlor."

Several years passed before public acceptance began to build, but by the 1880s, typewriters were becoming a standard office tool. Sales increased dramatically after 1887 when the visible typewriter was introduced, enabling the operator to see what was being printed while it was being typed.

The typewriter, along with the Edison Dictograph, which came into use about the same time, revolutionized the office and had an enormous social impact on the workplace. Just as in the computer revolution of the late 20th century, office workers had enormous difficulty accepting a radically new and different innovation. They were quite uncomfortable with something that could entirely change traditional work habits, and found the typewriter too hard to understand and use effectively. Prior to the typewriter, the labors of office secretaries, clerks, and bookkeepers were usually performed by men. An unintended consequence of the appearance of these new appliances in the office was the introduction of women into the workforce. While eschewing the new technology, men were strongly resistant to women assuming what had been a traditionally male-dominated occupation. Despite the obstacles, women readily embraced and adapted to the new contraptions. While initially only reluctantly accepted, women ultimately became entrusted with the responsibility for the operation of these costly and intricate instruments. It wasn't long before the woman in the office was considered the indispensable "Girl Friday."

For its size, the typewriter was certainly one of the most complex consumer machines manufactured in the 19th century. Entirely mechanical, the average typewriter could contain up to 2000 parts. Levers, pins, springs, gears, and a myriad assortment of other paraphernalia all worked together in precise concert to achieve the miracle of mechanized writing.

By 1905, nearly 2700 patents had been granted for typewriters and improvements in the United States alone. The robustness of the typewriter industry during its first half century is demonstrated by the fact that this history lists over 300 makers of typewriters.

The Typewriter Magazine, whose initial issue appeared in 1877, was the first journal to support and record the advances of the burgeoning industry. However, *Type-*

writer Topics, which began documenting the evolution and advances of the industry in September 1905, ultimately became the foremost periodical devoted exclusively to the subject, enjoying a circulation of nearly 13,000 by 1908.

Eighteen years after it's founding, *Typewriter Topics* published a comprehensive retrospective of the typewriter's first half century. While it was obviously biased towards the trade it chronicled, the issue celebrating the ". . . semi-centennial of the Founding of the Typewriter Industry" nonetheless provided a unique insight into the history of an enterprise by the people who made and participated in it. The interest in and popularity of the original article is evidenced by the appearance of this reprint with addenda less than a year later.

The editors proudly declared ". . . it [is] our earnest purpose to include every typewriter ever known . . ." This volume certainly affirms their attempt at comprehensiveness. In addition to discussing all the major typewriter pioneers, including Hammond, Blickensderfer, Oliver, Remington, L.C. Smith, Underwood, and Smith Premier, the editors also introduce us to many fascinating lesser-knowns and also-rans like the Yu Ess (as in U.S.), the Dactygam, the Dollar, and the Ford.

Although this semi-centenary narrative provides a wonderful window into the most interesting and exciting formative years of the typewriter, much of its history was yet to be written. Electric machines, for example, were still experimental at the time of publication. Even though Edison patented an electric typewriter in 1871 and a handful of others followed, it wasn't until the Blickensderfer Electric was commercially produced in 1902 that a workable model was available to consumers. More experimentation followed, but it would be 1921 before another practical electric, the Mercedes 'Electra' reached the market.

Sounding remarkably contemporary and upbeat, the editors in 1923 boasted that since 1873 ". . . the world has progressed more than it has . . . done in thousands of years. . . . the typewriter undoubtedly has been more instrumental in the world's progress than anything else. No longer is the writing machine in competition with the pen . . .

"The typewriter is ever expanding its field of utility . . . and the next fifty years will see an even greater development." Looking ahead, the editors confidently predicted: "The day will come when its utility in the home will be universally recognized. It will render obsolete the school room copybook for the child in learning his first lessons."

While much of their vision was realized, the editors could not know that this marvelous creation would have a finite life, eventually being supplanted by the computer. Seventy-five years after the original publication of the retrospective, the number of typewriter manufacturers had dwindled to 25 worldwide.

The once ubiquitous audible presence of typewriters has been all but silenced. Almost unheard today are the distinctive sounds of type striking platens, the end of line and paper bells, the catchy ratcheting of the line advance lever, and the peculiar sound of the carriage return. It probably will not be too many years before the typewriter becomes extinct—an anachronistic relic consigned to museums of industrial and technological design. It will go the way of the slide rule, the adding machine, and the phonograph.

Despite its wane, the legacy of the typewriter remains. Even the latest ergonomic computer keyboard owes its basic letter layout to the arcane "qwerty" system devised by C.L. Sholes. Much to the chagrin of more than a century-and-a-quarter of touch-typing students struggling to memorize the difficult character arrangement, this was merely a sequence that Sholes implemented to avoid troublesome mechanical conflicts and interference between frequently used letters. Introduced in 1872, it has remained the virtually unchanged standard ever since. "Shift," "Tab," and "Backspace" are also carryover terms from the earliest typewriters.

It is surprising that a very small body of work exists for such an historic innovation as the typewriter. Therefore, this volume, which was primarily intended for those within the trade and today is an exceedingly scarce publication, should prove especially valuable to historians and collectors. For anyone even casually interested in the evolution of this remarkable machine, the score of illustrations, along with company biographies and fifty-eight paid advertisements will provide fascinating insights into the state of the art as it existed in 1924.

Today, more than 125 years after the typewriter's introduction, we are left with only the ghosts of these wonderful early examples of ingenuity and industrial technology. It is the intent of this reprint to serve as a tribute to the machine that "superseded the pen."

NB. This edition is a faithful reproduction of the original. As a result, all of the quirks and typographical errors of the original are included, reflecting the informality of the era. For example, under the "R" listings, Remington is found out of sequence.

Victor M. Linoff

Selected Bibliography and Recommended Further Reading

Beeching, Wilfred A. *Century of the Typewriter.* Bournemouth, Dorset, England: British Typewriter Museum Publishing, 1974 (1990 printing).

Bliven Jr., Bruce. *The Wonderful Writing Machine.* New York: Random House, 1954.

Current, Richard N. *The Typewriter and The Men Who Made It.* Arcadia, CA: Post-Era Books, 1954 (1988 second edition).

Mares, G.C. *History of the Typewriter: Successor to the Pen.* Arcadia, CA: Post-Era Books, 1985 (Reprint of the original 1909 edition).

THE
TYPEWRITER

History & Encyclopedia

REPRINTED EDITION

From the October, 1923, issue of
TYPEWRITER TOPICS
The International Office
Equipment Magazine

With
Addenda

PRICE ONE DOLLAR

GEYER'S STATIONER AND
BUSINESS EQUIPMENT *TOPICS*

International Trade Journal of Office Equipment

260 FIFTH AVE., NEW YORK, N. Y.

One Man Tells Another

Over one hundred thousand Woodstock Typewriters have been placed in the hands of satisfied users. What one user has told another has played no small part in this achievement. It is needless to say that the Woodstock Typewriter Company can do nothing to harm this reputation.

Woodstock Typewriter Company, Chicago, Ill., U. S. A.

Shannotype

Simple Production - - - - - -
- - - - - - - Perfect Results

Shannotyped letters are *personal letters.*

They appear worth reading and are read when duplicated work is passed over with a glance.

Shannotype work is indistinguishable from typewriting because it is produced on the same principle, and yet the complete equipment, including Type-setter, 4,000 type, tools, etc., costs only what it will save in results on a single circularizing campaign of 20,000.

Specimens of Shannotype work and a descriptive leaflet will be sent on application, or a demonstration will be arranged by appointment.

"Shannon Corner"
57-59, VICTORIA STREET
LONDON, S.W.1

THE Shannon
LIMITED

50ᵗʰ Anniversary
of the Typewriter

Christopher Latham Sholes, inventor of the typewriter, at work on one of his experimental machines (1872)

Cut from the first typewriter catalogue (1874). This picture was prophetic of the millions of women who have since earned their living through the writing machine

·1873·
Model 1
Remington

There was no such word as "Typewriter" until Remington made the first one fifty years ago.

·1923·
Quiet 12
Remington

Remington still the last word in Typewriters

Remington Typewriter Company, 374 Broadway, New York—Branches Everywhere

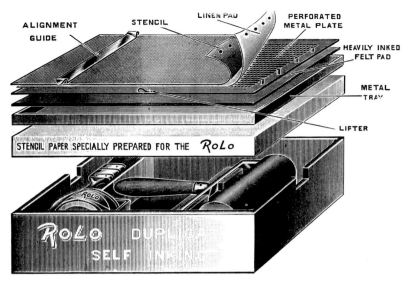

THE

SELF INKING
DUPLICATOR

Fifteen hundred perfect facsimile hand or typewritten copies within one hour can be run off on the Rolo Duplicator, without practically any preparation.

The Rolo is ready charged with ink for use, and will reproduce upwards of 1,500 copies without replenishing with ink.

The Stencil Sheet is cut in the usual manner by the Typewriter, or by hand, adjusted to the machine, after which some thousands of copies can be taken.

There are no complicated adjustments, and copies can be taken as quickly as 25 per minute by an unskilled operator.

The outfit is supplied in handsome metal case, with all accessories ready for use, including stencil paper, ink, brush, rubber roller, alignment guide, etc.

QUARTO SIZE 8″ x 10″	**55s.**
F'CAP SIZE 8″ x 13″	**75s.**
BRIEF SIZE 13″ x 16″	**95s.**

ROLOSKIN

The new Dry Type Indestructible Stencil Paper.

This stencil will yield 10,000 or more perfect copies from a single sheet, and does not require dampening before use. *Samples and prices on application.*

RoLo, Ltd., 40, HOLBORN VIADUCT, LONDON. E.C.1, ENGLAND

A CONDENSED HISTORY OF THE WRITING MACHINE

❖

The Romance of Earlier Effort and the Realities of Present Day Accomplishment

❖

Compiled in Celebration of the Semi-Centennial of the Founding of the Typewriter Industry

A PATENT was granted by Queen Anne to Henry Mill, an English engineer, in 1713 for an invention described as "an artificial machine for the impressing or transcribing of letters singly or progressively one after another as in writing." The first recorded effort to build a writing machine in America is found in a patent issued by the United States Patent Office in 1829 to William A. Burt of Detroit, Michigan. Xavier Projean, of Marseilles, France, built a machine in 1833 with type bars which struck downward in something like the fashion of a few typewriters of later day. Guiseppe R a v i z z a, an Italian, completed a workable device for mechanical writing in 1856.

Particularly in years following the last mentioned, many patents for mechanical writing machines were issued. In this magazine since its start almost twenty years ago, there has been printed numerous narratives of early inventions which never reached the state of manufacture. The story has been told in these columns by text and illustrations of the first commercially successful result when in 1873 the "t y p e - w r i t e r" of C. Latham Sholes was actually first manufactured for sale to the using public. That was 50 years ago and it was then that it can be said the typewriter industry was born.

THE BURT MACHINE OF 1829
Illustration from the September, 1905, issue of this magazine

The development of typewriting devices during the latter period is another story, a big and important story, collected and presented in this special 50th Anniversary Number in condensed form but from broadly separated and many sources. Fragmentary details have been secured from past issues of this magazine and acknowledgment is made of valued assistance by men of prominence in the industry who have freely acquainted us with facts herein presented for the first time in any publication. Not many attempts have heretofore been made to cover the subject completely, though a number of different compilations have currently described the typewriters existant at the time and a few have presented the more aged inventions. What is undoubtedly the most serious and praiseworthy attempt was by Ernst Martin, of Germany, who published in 1920 a very exhaustive description in book form of many different makes and models. By text and illustration he qualifies as a typewriter historian of first rank and by the addition of another volume just published covering products introduced since the period embraced by the initial volume he

strengthens his position as an authority on writing machines.

Many will remember the activity of the F. S. Webster Company many years ago as typewriter dealers, handling all makes through their offices in Boston, New York, Chicago, Pittsburgh and London; 100 pages of a book written by Frank E. Kneeland and published in 1898 was a complete catalog of its day and deserves mention as a compilation now historical. Charles E. Weller, a former telegraph operator and shorthand writer, of La Porte, Indiana, wrote an absorbingly interesting book entitled "The Early History of the Typewriter" which tells of his contact with the inventor and the trials of early Sholes models. We possess a copy of a little booklet published by E. N. Miner, proprietor of T y p e w r i t e r Headquarters, es-

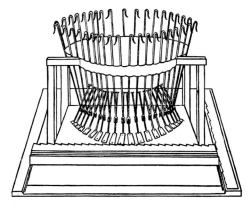

DRAFTSMAN'S CONCEPTION OF THE TYPEBAR CONSTRUCTION OF THE PROJEAN MACHINE OF 1833

Supplied for this historical compilation by C. V. Oden

tablished in 1883, and written when he was located at 102 Fulton Street in New York; it carried a number of illuminating illustrations and descriptions.

The book written by Carl Mares is worthy of high commendation as a typewriter history and covered in its contents at the time of publication in 1909 a very excellent compilation; it was published by Guilbert Pitman & Company of London. Conte Emilo Budan, of Venice, Italy, was likewise the author of a book on antique typewriters in which important records were established. Charles W. Howell, of the Sun Typewriter Company in New York, is a fountain head of information particularly in reference to patent rights. R. W. Uhlig possesses numerous remembrances of happenings of note. And Wm. H. Beardsley, 40 years consecutively in the business and at present head of the General Typewriter Exchange at Brooklyn, N. Y., is probably the best conversationalist in the industry in relation to human interest recollections.

C. V. Oden, of the Underwood Typewriter Co., is an exceptionally well posted man on mechanical constructions and

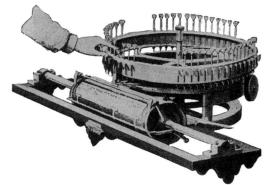

THE THURBER MACHINE OF 1843
Illustration through courtesy of the Remington Typewriter Company

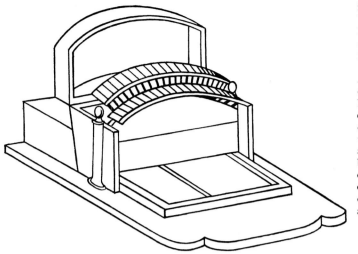

THE ABOVE ILLUSTRATES THE FRAME OF THE
FOUCAULD MACHINE OF 1843

Drawing by courtesy of C. V. Oden

he has written much of value; he has collected material from many sources and possesses in written form and mental knowledge more than enough to qualify him as an authority on typewriter history. A. C. Reiley, advertising manager of the Remington Typewriter Company, even though he would modestly disclaim such designation, is known to possess historical data amply justifying placing his name in the list of historians of the typewriter industry. J. E. Thomas, president of the long existing Typewriter Inspection Company of New York and himself an inventor of proven foresight, is intimately acquainted with much that has transpired in growth and development of the typewriter industry. "Typewriters in Germany" was the subject of an article in the May, 1906, issue of "TOPICS" by A. Beyerlen, of Stuttgart, Germany, which, though brief, stamped him as an historian well acquainted with the marketing of typewriters in Europe. And the several contributions to this trade paper by R. F. Howard, at the time they were written in 1905 a member of the editorial staff of a Milwaukee newspaper and personal friend of C. Latham Sholes, conveyed information and insight into early obstacles confronted in preparation of the first commercially successful writing machine.

The Royal Typewriter Company issued in 1921 a book on "The Evolution of the Typewriter" which illustrated a number of the older typewriters upon which patents were issued by the United States Patent Office. "Photographs by permission of the Smithsonian Institute, Washington, D. C." appeared under very excellent illustrations of several old machines, indicating special grant given for reproduction of models on permanent display at the National Museum. Through the courtesy of that company, we were given permission to use the same pictures

in this historical compilation, those so utilized herein being identified by the same caption. Credit of a more personal nature for collection of the material contained in the booklet here mentioned is due E. B. Hess, inventor of the Royal and a patent expert of note in typewriter circles.

As an example of typewriter history the volume reviewed in August, 1923, "TOPICS," entitled "The Story of the Typewriter," commands a prominent place. It is the latest publication of the kind to come from the presses and is of especial importance because it was prepared in commemoration of the 50th anniversary of the birth of the writing machine industry celebrated in eventful manner at Ilion, New York, on September 12th. Under the auspices of the Herkimer County Historical Society both the book was published and celebration held at the spot from whence came the first factory built writing machine in 1873. To large degree for the purpose of extending that celebration to cover the entire industry and in demonstration of full accord with the date as marking the beginning of serious typewriter manufacture, this issue of "TOPICS" is dedicated as an appropriate trade vehicle for commemoration of the Semi-Centennial of the Typewriter Industry. The 50th birthday of any industry justifies a perpetuating celebration. In brief resumé, it is our rare and appreciated privilege to present the earlier efforts and a half-century of manufacturing history now completed by the great and growing typewriter industry.

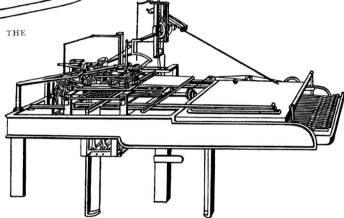

ILLUSTRATION OF THE EDDY MACHINE OF 1850—FROM THE COLLEC
TION OF C. V. ODEN

THE FAIRBANKS PHONETIC WRITER OF 1850

*Photograph by permission of the Smithsonian Institution, Washington,
D. C., Museum No. 251,212, and illustrated here by courtesy of the Royal
Typewriter Company*

THE HUGHES WRITING MACHINE OF 1850

*On exhibition at the Science Museum at South
Kensington, London, England*

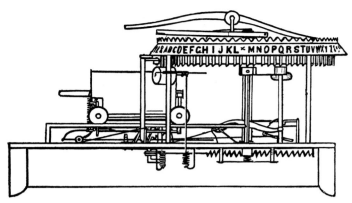

DRAWING OF THE JONES MACHINE, 1852—BY COURTESY OF
C. V. ODEN

There is a tremendously interesting story in what took place prior to the advent of a practical machine for mechanical writing which cannot be given in its entirety here, of course, but which, nevertheless, is deserving of review in advance of the narrative of inventions belonging to the era which this special issue celebrates. All effort in earlier years reflects the realization that methods of writing were laborious, this including the entire evolution from hieroglyphics down to the pen made of steel. Seventy years ago in a word speed contest, reflecting the tendency towards greater speed, Miss Lillian Wrighter won over Miss Helen West by writing an average of thirty words per minute with her pen.

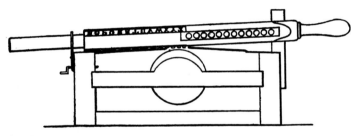

AN IDEA OF THE THOMAS MACHINE FROM THE HISTORICAL FILE
OF C. V. ODEN—AN INVENTION OF 1854

The saving of time was rapidly being realized as paramount, and it was acknowledged many decades ago that no invention would save more time in essential pursuits than would a mechanical writing machine. Hence the expenditure of effort covering more than a hundred years which helped to lay the foundation for successes in the present generation. Dreams of mechanical means for making writing universally legible and less burdensome were made realities through the labors of pioneers whose then impractical ideas had much to do with the perfection of the modern business tool of today.

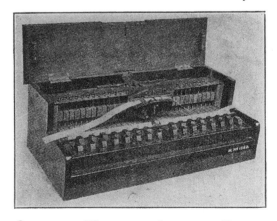

ONE OF THE WHEATSTONE INVENTIONS DATING
FROM 1851 TO 1862
*On exhibition at the Science Museum at South
Kensington, London, England*

In the first paragraph of this narrative the outstanding events of public record in four countries are mentioned, but there were many others who contributed to the history of typewriter invention during the years prior to advent in 1873 of the acknowledged first writing machine successfully marketed.

Work was done between the years 1753 to 1760 on a writing machine by one Von Knaus of Vienna, Austria.

There is small record of a machine made by Count Reipperg of Vienna, Austria, in 1762.

Louis Jacquet, a Swiss, residing in Neuenburg, Germany, is identified as a writing machine inventor in about 1780.

A writing machine for the blind was invented by a Frenchman named Pingeron in 1780.

ILLUSTRATION REPRODUCED FROM THE NOVEMBER, 1905,
ISSUE OF THIS INTERNATIONAL TRADE PAPER—AN
INVENTION OF 1856

A machine writing all caps was built in 1808 for the blind Countess Carolina Fantoni da Fivizzono by Pellegrino Turri di Castelnuovo. This is really the first effort that can be called a machine, all previous devices being ordinary apparatus depending much on hand manipulation.

Pietro Conti of Cilavegna built a machine in 1823, claiming at the time that it "wrote fast and clear enough for anyone, even those with bad sight." The Conti machine was put before the Academie Francaise and eventually sold for 600 francs.

THE JOHN H. COOPER WRITING MACHINE OF 1856
*Photograph by permission of the Smithsonian Institution, Washington,
D. C., National Museum No. 251,211, and reproduced from illustration
furnished by the Royal Typewriter Company*

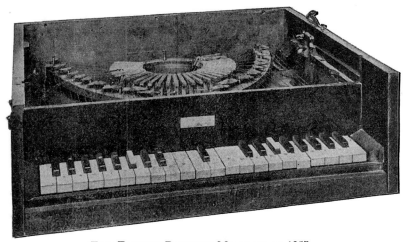

THE FRANCIS PRINTING MACHINE OF 1857

Photograph by permission of the Smithsonian Institution, Washington, D. C., National Museum No. 180,060, and shown here by courtesy of the Royal Typewriter Company

Giuseppe Ravizza, a lawyer of Novara, Italy, who had been interested in mechanical writing since 1830, began working on his "Cembalo-scrivano" in 1837. He produced the nearest thing to what was later called the typewriter and by far the best device of its kind invented up until that time. Ravizza continued to work on writing machines until his death in 1885. In all he made 12 different models of machines. The first prospectus on typewriters ever printed was gotten out by this pioneer inventor in 1856, the price upon his machine mentioned therein being placed at 300 lire. Numbers of the machines which Ravizza constructed are said to have been sold by him. The principal patents were issued on September 1, 1855, and March 31, 1856, a machine having been exhibited, among other places, at the Exhibition of Turin in 1858 where it was awarded a silver medal. The most striking feature of the Rivizza machine, called by the inventor the "writing cymbal," interpreted into English, was the typebar basket with 32 bars almost exactly in constructive detail like modern typewriters. There was also developed the step by step movement of the carriage given by a very original escapement, and two systems of inking; one by aid of a fabric ribbon imbibed with coloring matter, having a lengthwise and up and down movement, and another with an inking roller. As said in the alphabetical classifications of modern inventions, the Olivetti people, first to make typewriters in Italy in commercial quantities, are proud of the fact that there exists so purely an Italian pedigree in creation of writing instruments as the Ravizza invention.

The first American writing machine, made by William Austin Burt, of Detroit, Michigan, appeared in 1829. This device was called the "Typograph," looked as much like a meat block in a butcher shop as anything with which it can be likened and was operated by a lever connected with a circular frame which carried the type.

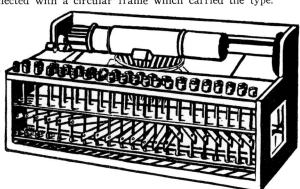

THE ILLUSTRATIVE RECORD OF THE HOUSE TYPEWRITER FROM THE ARCHIVES OF C. V. ODEN—1865 WAS ITS YEAR

A pointer or indicator at the end of this box-like affair corresponded with the position of the type on the frame inside the box and when in proper position the type were depressed into contact with the platen. The principle of feeding the paper through the machine was similar to that in present use, except that there was nothing automatic about it. This machine was built entirely of wood. A drawing of the Burt contrivance accompanies this story.

A device called the "Ktypograph" constituted the first invention of a machine of the key lever type and was the product of the ingenious mind of Xavier Projean, its birth being in 1833. The type lay in a basket and were pulled against the paper by a lever key, but the paper did not move, the type mechanism changing position much as the present-day Elliott-Fisher flat surface machines are operated. M. Projean was a Frenchman, a printer in Marseilles. We show a drawing of the typebar construction of the Projean machine.

Jaan Jaackson, of Riga, Russia, devised a writing appliance which consisted of a calotte or semi-sphere formed of curved ribs each of which bore a series of printing characters or type. At the center of the calotte and above it was a handle whereby the device could be manipulated. In using it, the device was held by the

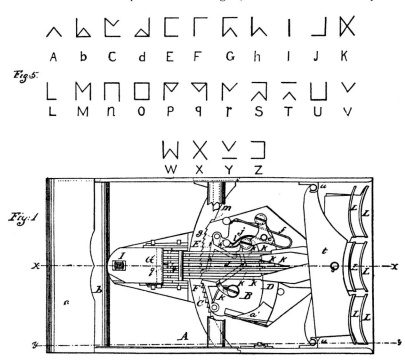

THE LIVERMORE PRINTING DEVICE OF 1863

Character combinations and patent drawing reproduced from the U. S. Patent Office Gazette Publication

handle and rolled upon a concave inking pad, the calotte being then turned about until the character desired was undermost, when it was impressed upon the paper. It was an appliance absolutely without value, an impractical invention for which we are unable to locate the date as to when it was devised.

A writing apparatus with 26 keys like on a piano was constructed in 1838 by M. Dujardin of Lille, France.

Louis Jerome Perrot, a Frenchman of Rouen, secured a patent in 1839 on a writing machine with characters reproduced from an upright cylinder.

Also in 1839, the machine of the famous Baron von Drais, a bicycle manufacturer, attracted no small amount of attention. It contained sixteen square keys.

In about 1840 Baillet de Sondalo & Coré, of Paris, invented machines that used an indicator with the left hand over the manipulating keyboard while the right hand brought the paper into contact with the type cylinder.

About 1841, Alexander Bain and Thomas Wright developed a machine for writing Morse characters for telegraphic purposes.

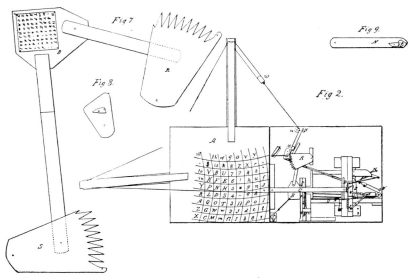

PEELER WRITING AND PRINTING MACHINE—1866
Photograph from the U. S. Patent Office Gazette

A machine working on the principle of devices often seen in places of amusement which emboss letters on strips of aluminum was built and patented in 1843 by Charles Thurber of Worcester, Mass. It had a movable carriage, which could be shifted in both directions, and a key for spacing between words, the spacing for letters being automatic. For line spacing the carriage was moved by hand the distance between holes on a slide bar. The keys and type, however, were all mounted on a large wheel, which in turn worked on the principle just mentioned, only instead of having one handle for all the letters each type had a key of its own adopted to being forced down against the paper. A model of this machine, called the "Chirographer," is preserved by the Smithsonian Institute at Washington, D.C. A later model substituted a flat platen for a round one, into which the paper could be fed longitudinally. A very good picture of the earlier Thurber machine is a feature of this special number.

Then came the machine by the blind Frenchman, Pierre Foucault, of Corbeil, in 1843, called the "Raphigraphe" and for use by the blind. This was followed later by his "Clavier Imprimeur" for regular use, a machine which was publicly described in 1850. A memory drawing of the frame of this machine is shown.

Somewhere between 1843 and 1850 the machines of Prof. William Hughes and Marchesi came into being only to disappear without record of detail.

The next discoveries recorded by historians whose findings have been searched out for review in this special issue are the machines of Henry Pape, Paris; Labrunie de Nerval, Paris; Littledale, of York (1844), and the apparatus of Dr. Saintard and Saint-Gilles in 1845. Then followed Prentice in 1847 with a machine about which also no details are available.

Another machine to be added to the list of early efforts is that of the Frenchman, Gustave Froment, whose model was built and put on display at the Musée of Arts and Metiers, Paris, in 1847.

In 1850, Oliver T. Eddy, of Baltimore, Md., built a machine "designed to furnish the means of substituting printed letters and signs for written ones in the transaction of every-day business." It was a cumbersome and complicated mechanism, having 78 type bars distributed over 13 vertical rows, like on a piano keyboard, as can be seen in the illustration.

J. B. Fairbanks, also in 1850, received a patent at the U. S. Patent Office for his typewriter invention, its description indicating that it was a phonetic writer as well as a calico printer. As the illustration verifies, the Fairbanks invention looked little like a writing machine.

A typewriter for the blind was invented in 1850 by G. A. Hughes, head of a blind institution of Manchester, England. While the first produced embossed letters only, a later model was designed for ordinary printing. The

Hughes machine had the type on a wheel which occupied a horizontal position from which pressure downward made the impression. We show a picture of this ancient invention.

John M. Jones, of Clyde, New York, brought out a creation in 1852 which, in the absence of any knowledge of the present designating term, was called by him a "Mechanical Typographer." The research work by E. B. Hess, of the Royal Typewriter Co., develops the fact that this device showed the first use of vertical figures and characters on a revolving disk and embodied the first cylindrical platen and line space ratchet and lever control. The patent drawing reproduced herewith gives an idea of the Jones machine, which really did exceptionally nice work.

In 1854 a writing machine named the "Typograph" by the inventor was devised by R. S. Thomas, of Wilmington, North Carolina, a patent being granted to cover his idea. A rather unsatisfactory illustration gives very little insight into the character of the Thomas invention.

The work on writing machines from 1851 to 1860 by Charles Wheatstone is also noted. The model of his machine, which we illustrate, had 29 keys; it was a complicated mechanism.

John Cooper's machine was devised in Philadelphia in 1856, it being a large device. Its impression was made by a hammer blow against a wheel or disk. It had a rotatable cylindrical platen with rolls for feeding the paper. A picture of this machine is shown.

A patent was granted to A. E. Beach in 1856 upon the first writing machine which combined the keys into a bank, with the type all striking at a common center and an escapement by means of a common connection. The machine was designed for the purpose of writing embossed letters on strips of paper for the blind. It wrote capitals as well as small letters and looked not unlike some machines later placed on the market. A subsequent model made by Alfred Beach was adopted to ordinary writing. An illustration gives an excellent idea of this top strike, typebar, ribbon writing device.

JOHN PRATT'S "PTEROTYPE" OF 1868
Photograph by permission of the Smithsonian Institution, Washington, D. C., National Museum No. 181,126, and shown by kindness of the Royal Typewriter Company

Samuel W. Francis, a doctor of medicine in New York, invented a "Printing Machine" in 1857 which embodied mechanical construction providing for a common printing center. It was followed by several later models. The keyboard resembled a piano, had 36 keys and a shift for capitals. The machine was priced at $100, no doubt the earliest instance of a writing machine being quoted at the figure so universally accepted in later years. This machine is also illustrated.

History records an effort to make a "Mechanical Typographer" by Henry Harger in the year 1858.

The authority quoted previously records machines by Guillemont, Paris (1859), Codvelle-La Basée (1861) and a machine in 1863 by Flamm that even wrote syllables.

F. A. de May, of New York, is said to have conceived his idea of a "Printing Apparatus" in 1863, a machine similar to Thurber's.

Also in 1863, Benjamin Livermore, of Hartford, Vermont, contributed a machine to the list of typewriter inventions. Its novelty was character signs, used singly or in combinations to form the letters. (See illustration).

Peter Mitterhofer's machine appeared in 1864, a device made to perforate characters on paper. Two years later this inventor, who lived in Tyrol, brought out another machine which was priced at 80 Kr. A third model was sold to the Polytechnic Institute in Vienna for 60 Kr.

In 1865, George House, of Buffalo, New York, contributed a machine marking a rather significant contribution to early development. As can be seen in the line drawing herewith, the type were arranged on bars which hung in a basket and struck upward against the platen at a common printing center. The principle employed was a forerunner of others operating similarly and later manufactured for public consumption.

The year 1866 is marked by the invention of "a machine for writing and printing," by Abner Peeler, of Webster City, Iowa. It had 81 characters, and, while not readily understandable to the laymen, a reproduction of the patent drawing is shown in conjunction with this brief description of the earlier writing machine patents.

In 1866, the "Pterotype" of John Pratt, of Centre, Alabama, was invented, a machine of which considerable has been said from time to time. It was patented in England and models made for

THE PASTOR HANSEN SCHREIBKUGEL, OR WRITING SPHERE, OF 1872
Photograph by permission of the Smithsonian Institution, Washington, D. C., National Museum No. 181,005. Illustration from the collection made by the Royal Typewriter Company

the inventor by E. B. Burge of London. One of the earlier models of Pratt's machine is in the Victoria and Albert Museum of London. He developed several different models and it is not known whether that is the first one he made. The illustration we use is of the machine patented in the United States in 1868.

R. Allen's machine in 1867 claimed to be "much faster than the pen" and the machine of Fontaine, of Paris, with 47 keys wrote through a ribbon.

A Brazilian Priest, Francisco Jano de Avézedo, is supposed to have invented a writing machine. The model was constructed of wood and was later to be made of metal. This machine was displayed in Pernambuco in 1867 and although awarded a medal the inventor was unable to secure financial assistance in producing machines.

In 1867, Thomas Hall, of Brooklyn, New York, made the first of the machines bearing his name and which had a more or less broad sale in later years.

The author of the typewriter history published in Germany, Ernst Martin, devotes considerable space in his book to a machine which, translated into English, was named the "Writing Sphere," from the fact that it was shaped something like a half-globe. In some respects it was not unlike the Foucault machine, the first model being a writing device for the blind. Pastor Hans Rasmus Malling Johan Hansen, of Copenhagen, said to have been a minister of the Lutheran church, was the inventor of the "Schreibkugel," claimed by Mr. Martin to have been the first machine regularly manufactured for sale to the public. It was originally designed for the blind but the principle was later applied to a machine for business use. The heavy carriage of the machine interfered with its speed, but the use of electromagnetic action applied to the sector of the "Writing Sphere" eased it considerably. The machine sold for 400 Kr. in Denmark and 600 Gulden in Austria for the electric machine, but these prices were found to be too high at that time for satisfactory merchandising. Its year of classification is 1872. It was patented in the United States on April 23 of that year. An excellent picture of Pastor Hansen's machine is shown.

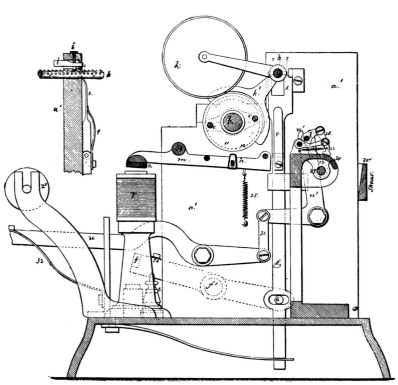

PHOTOGRAPHED FROM PATENT DRAWING IN THE U. S. PATENT OFFICE GAZETTE, ILLUSTRATING THE THOS. A. EDISON PATENT OF 1872

THE SHOLES, GLIDDEN & SOULE TYPEWRITING MACHINE—PATENTED ON
JUNE 23, 1868

*Photograph by permission of the Smithsonian Institution, Washington,
D. C., National Museum No. 251,210. Cut supplied by the Royal Typewriter Company*

Thomas Edison is given credit by some historians of the typewriter as the inventor of an electric wheel device introduced in
1872 which is claimed to have been the foundation for the
present-day printing mechanism of stock tickers.

The first model of the Sholes, Glidden and Soule machine
patented in 1868 and from which developed the Remington typewriter in 1873 is in the Smithsonian Institute at Washington, as
is also the second one constructed in the same year. Photographs
of both of these machines are shown in this narrative leading
up to the actual birth of the typewriter industry 50 years ago
which is celebrated by this historical semi-centennial number.

In the current news section of this historical number there is a
big story about the 50th birthday celebration held at Ilion,
New York, on September 12 under the auspices of the Herkimer
County Historical Society. While there was much brought to
light then in portrayal of the struggles of the Remingtons and
their associates to make of the invention of Christopher Latham
Sholes a commercially successful and marketable product,
no inconsiderable amount of the interest of those who
attended the Ilion celebration was attracted because of
the revival of earlier memories.

Almost twenty years ago this trade paper printed the
picture reproduced below. The photograph was taken in
1872 and shows the daughter of the inventor seated at
one of the various models built by Mr. Sholes. Her interest in the work of
her illustrious parent
was vividly recalled
and she made a
prominent figure in
typewriter history
through participation
in the Ilion celebra-
tion, which she at-
tended in company
with her husband.
The Miss Sholes
who is pictured
herewith is now
Mrs. Charles L. For-
tier, with whom
Christopher Latham
Sholes lived during
the last years of his
life. This picture of
the first woman who
ever wrote on a

DAUGHTER OF SHOLES SEATED AT
ONE OF HIS EARLY MODELS

typewriter was pro-
phetic of the mil-
lions of woman who
have since earned
their livelihood on
the writing machine.

Another event of
the Ilion celebration
which rightly be-
longs in this histori-
cal compilation was
the unveiling of a
bronze tablet in
memory of Chris-
topher Latham
Sholes. This was
affixed to a monu-
mental stone erected
in Sholes Park, a
plot near the Rem-
ington typewriter
factory dedicated to

CHRISTOPHER LATHAM SHOLES

the inventor. Elizabeth Latham Sholes and Christopher
Latham Sholes 4th, great grandchildren of the famous
Sholes, uncovered the commemorating monument in-
scribed in wording found in the current story of the
Ilion celebration and erected by the Herkimer County
Historical Society.

Charles E. Weller, who was the first typewriter operator, was likewise a conspicuous figure at the 50th birthday party of the commercial typewriter. In 1868 when Christopher
Latham Sholes completed his first workable model he sent it to
his friend Weller for practical testing. Mr. Weller, then resident
in St. Louis, tested out this and subsequent Sholes machines in
connection with his profession of official shorthand reporter.

THE PAST FIFTY YEARS

By way of explanatory introduction to the following portion
of this issue, treating inventions since the birth of the typewriter
industry in 1873, we wish to call attention to the fact that in many
cases the different names under which the same or similar machine
has been known are usually included under the one heading of
chief importance. No attempt has been made, nor was it necessary, to unduly inflate the paragraphed references in order to
convey a true picture of the great writing machine industry.

THE SHOLES, GLIDDEN & SOULE TYPEWRITER—PATENTED ON JULY 14, 1868
Illustration from an issue of this trade paper in 1905

Brevity and conciseness have governed the writing of the story, it being our earnest purpose to include every typewriter ever known, regardless of the degree of success which attended its introduction into the field. That something should be overlooked, however, is quite inevitable in a compilation so extensive; the human element or failure to comply with requests for information are the only excuses for omission of data or illustrations which it was intended to include.

It was a temptation in preparation of this historical edition to embrace the many typewriter attachments of independent invention and offerings which have appeared from time to time in augmentation of the more complete contributions to writing machine development and improvement. But, like the impossibility of presenting a full record of all the typewriter patents ever issued, we were obliged to stop somewhere. As a consequence, such things as practice machines, tabulators, shorthand machines, music writers, accessories, etc., are omitted with no little regret. If the subject were carried to the length of one compiler who pictured and described a mechanical printer of figures as a logical companion to all machines that print from type, we could include the many adding and calculating machines which record on paper the results of arithmetical computations—a big and important story in itself which ambition may some day induce us to collect for publication in like manner to this issue.

Acme

It is appropriate that in alphabetical arrangement of the condensed history of typewriters which made their appearance during the fifty-year period to which his issue is especially dedicated that the Acme should occupy an early position following mention of C. Latham Sholes. The Acme was invented by Zalmon G. Sholes, a son of the elder inventor who is credited with having been responsible for the birth of the typewriter industry in 1873.

This machine was first named the "Waterbury Standard Visible" in a plan to identify the manufacture of typewriters with the city in which the owning company was located, Waterbury, Conn. The Zalmon G. Sholes Typewriter Company was organized in March, 1911, with capital stock of $1,000,000, by Waterbury men headed by John Moriarity, who was elected president. The original intention was to market the machine, later changed to the Acme, at a retail price of $50.

A. E. G.

The largest manufacturers of electrical goods in Germany, the Allgemeine Electrizitäts Ges., Berlin, are responsible for a venture into the production of a standard typewriter which looms with no little importance on the horizon of the industry. The subsidiary company actually operating in the writing machine field in introduction of this new typewriter was the A. E. G. Schreibmaschinen Gesellschaft, of Berlin, W. 66, but only in August of the current year that company amalgamated with the Deutsche Werke Aktiengesellschaft and a new company was formed for the purpose of greatly enlarging the output of A. E. G. typewriters. A. E. G. Deutsche Werke Schreibmaschinen G.m.b.H. is the official name of the new institution.

To the well-known General Electric Company of Germany, when they took up the A. E. G. in 1921, the manufacture of typewriters was not foreign, that company for twenty years having produced the Mignon typewriter, of which many were sold. The A. E. G. is a standard type of machine with practically every modern feature characteristic to single shift, 42-key machines. It has the knife blade bar, interchangeable carriage, tabulator, etc. The makers of the A. E. G. machine have been working on it since 1911 and although very nearly ready for the market in 1914 its appearance was interrupted by the war. It came out in 1921 in quite perfect manner. The construction has been tested and examined through many years in the works of this world-renowned firm. It has an appearance which has won many friends at home and abroad. Special features, apart from the symmetric arrangement of the keys and

the short type bars, are the space writing which makes the writing of particular words and phrases easier, and the carriage built after a new system which makes the shifting easier and sure. The carriage is constructed in such a way that it is transported on a steel bar without a special inner carriage with gliding studs, whereby the carriage is supported at its heaviest point by ball-bearings; this insures an absolutely perfect alignment of the writing.

The taking over of the works in Erfurt of the Deutsche Werke Aktiengesellschaft is going to increase the manufacture of their Mignon as well as that of the standard typewriter. The name of the firm after the fusion with the Erfurt works is given above, and Berlin, W. 66, Mauerstrasse 83/84, is the location of the general offices.

Adler

The fabrication of the Adler typewriter, the first German-made writing machine with the typebar system, was based upon the elementary patents of Wellington P. Kidder's invention of the

THE TRAVELING ADLER

horizontal push or forward thrust action. The principle of manufacturing a first-class machine only and adherence to the original type of mechanism has characterized all the years of Adler history. The regular Model 7, Model 8 with interchangeable type-sets for writing in different languages or characters, Model 11 with two different sets of type combined in one machine, Model 15 with one single shift key, Model 16 with single shift key and interchangeable type sets, Model 17 with single shift key and two different sets of type, Model 18 for writing invoices and Model 19 with 46 keys and 138 characters for writing mathematical formulas, constitute the line of Standard Adlers. For the miniature Adler, like in the foregoing, it can be said that it is a real business tool—not a toy in any respect. Of course the Adler machine can be supplied with any special attachment desired, such as column finder, decimal tabulator, extra wide carriages, etc.

There is no question about German industry, especially in metal products, having received great stimulus by the existence of Adlerwerke vorm, Heinrich Kleyer. Automobiles and other articles as mentioned later have contributed notably to development, but allegiance to the writing machine industry has not only meant much to the Adler institution but their connection with the busi-

ness forms no small part of the grand total of growth recorded in development of typewriters. The special section of the big Adler works in Frankfurt which is devoted to typewriter manufacture is an impressive illustration of heavy investment for supply of this modern business machine.

THE STANDARD ADLER MODEL WITH TABULATOR

Heinrich Kleyer, while with a Hamburg machinery importing firm, was attracted to American products of that character. In 1879 he crossed the Atlantic and after employment in several factories to gain experience, returned to Germany to start the making of bicycles in Frankfort a. M. Success in that line and in the manufacturing of other articles led to adoption of a typewriter, for which manufacture began in 1898. The Adler typewriter dates from that time as the product of the Adler Fahrradwerke vorm. Heinrich Kleyer. It practically duplicated the Empire of Canadian origin and Kidder patent.

Various models of the Adler have been made, including No. 14 especially built for billing work. The 100,000th machine was passed in June, 1913, the past ten years recording many refinements leading up to the present standard model. In the same month when 100,000 of the big Adlers had been reached, a traveling model was introduced which has been called the Kleine Adler. It was made in like design to the large machine and has duplicated the success of the latter in manufacture and marketing. The Kleine Adler machine has been sold in Italy as the Adler-Piccola, in Spain as the Adlerita, in France as the Adlerette and in England as the Blick.

Albertson

A folding typewriter was invented by E. H. Albertson, of Fairfield, Conn., and the Albertson Folding Typewriter Company of the same place organized and start made to find capital in October, 1912.

Albus

This machine was made by Maschinenfabrik Carl Engler G.m.b.H., Vienna, Austria, making its appearance on the market in 1910 as the Engler.

The Albus was a folding typewriter of portable class and the forerunner of the Perkeo typewriter made by Clemens Müller G.m.b.H., of Dresden, Germany.

Alexander

The history of the Alexander typewriter was marked by troubles of the inventor and the company formed and licensed to make and sell the machine. Court actions comprise most of the review since first heard of in Endicott, N. Y., in 1907. A reorganization during the summer of that year of the Alexander Typewriter Company was in anticipation of moving to Kansas City, Mo., but the machine next figures in the organization of the United States Typewriter Co., East New York, Long Island, in January, 1908. In March, 1914, another or the former Alex-

ander Typewriter Company had a factory at 126 Atkins Avenue, Brooklyn, N. Y., where it was proposed to manufacture this invention of Jesse Alexander. This inventor was next heard of in England after the World War, his connection at that time being with a famous British munitions works who proposed the manufacture of another Alexander invention, a four-bank, single shift, lightweight typewriter.

Allen

Named in abbreviation of the city in which it is made, the Allen typewriter was invented by Richard W. Uhlig and has been manufactured at Allentown, Pa., since December, 1918, by the Allen Typewriter Company, of which James K. Bowen, a prominent capitalist of that city, is president. It has two shifts, 29 keys and 87 characters, the latest model, No. 9, having been on the market since 1921.

The entire construction of the Allen bespeaks simplicity and standardization of production. The frame is of cold rolled steel, the segment of a special non-corrodable metal, the key levers of a special aluminum alloy and all other parts of steel selected and tempered for its particular use. Particularly efficient is the back spacer, ribbon feeding mechanism, line locking and spacing mechanism. The Allen weighs less than 11½ pounds, takes paper 9 7/16 inches wide and writes a line 8¼ inches long. It uses a standard ½-inch bichrome ribbon.

Richard Uhlig, the inventor, first took his ideas for the Allen typewriter to James K. Bowen, a capitalist of Allentown, Pa., in July, 1917. Mr. Bowen was attracted by the simplicity of the typewriter and the thought that the three rows would be the ultimate keyboard arrangement for both speed and efficiency. Room was secured in a building at Fifth and Lawrence streets, Allentown, where the first working model was developed in 1918. In 1920 all activities were transferred to the company's new modern factory at Tenth and Turner streets, Allentown, the present quarters. During this time Models 1 to 10 were developed and a few of each sold to test them out under actual working conditions. These are still giving satisfaction.

The Allen is presented as a complete typewriter at a popular price. It is claimed for it that only 630 pieces do any and all of the work done by machines with many more pieces in their make-up. Development and refinement of factory methods are now completed and aggressive production and sales efforts are about to begin.

Richard Uhlig has been identified with the development of the typewriter for over fifty years. During this time he helped develop several of the present well-known makes. The Allen represents his best ideas for simplicity, strength of working parts and positive actions. James K. Bowen has likewise long been interested in encouraging the perfection of new ideas, as shown by his many successful business interests.

Amata

The first standard typewriter of Austrian manufacture was presented to the trade only as recently as in the last number of this international magazine, where a complete and detailed description of the Amata appears. It is manufactured in their own mechanical workshops by the long established and well-known engineering firm of J. von Petravic & Co., Vienna XVII, Schadinagasse 6-8. The Amata has the distinction of arrival just in time to appear in this historical classification.

The manufacturers outline to us the following particulars of the Amata typewriter: in provision of all features of a modern

THE AMATA TYPEWRITER, MADE IN AUSTRIA

machine it has a single shift with shift lock, removable platen, three-line spacings, locking of the keyboard and release, bell signal, two-color ribbon and stencil cutting equipment, automatic ribbon reverse, tabulator with automatic carriage brake, back spacer, normal keyboard with 44 keys for 88 characters and writing all civilized languages, a.s.f.

American

This was an indicator type of machine upon first appearance in 1893, with a semi-circular type carrier and keyboard scale. It was low priced and wrote 71 characters, selling under the name

given in the United States and as the Globe in Europe. Although bearing the same name this machine is not to be confused with the later appearing, more serviceable and business-like American typewriter, though they were both made by the same manufacturer. The indicator machine was not qualified to turn out work with speed, surpassing pen writing only in the fact that its work was in type. It had a type-wheel, ink roll, measured 4 x 7 x 11 inches, weighed 5 lbs. in its carrying case, was visible writing and had but 35 parts. Two models were made, both selling at $10.

In 1899 the machine of the type illustrated was first made and put out experimentally; in 1901 it was put actively on the market. At first it was made in the Williams factory at Derby, Conn., but in 1908 the company occupied its own plant at Bridgeport, Conn., at which time the last visible writing Model 8 made its appearance. This first of typebar machines to sell at $50 retail in America was sold elsewhere under a variety of names: Herald in France; Elgin, Favorit and Europa in Germany, and in England as the Fleet. It had 27 keys, wrote 81 characters, had double shift and wrote through a ribbon.

The manufacturers were the American Typewriter Company, with general offices for many years at 265 Broadway, New York City, and organized in the year when the first machines were marketed by Halbert E. Payne, who was president until the company made an assignment in August, 1915, and the American typewriter enterprise ceased to exist. Shortly following this, Mr.

Payne was commissioned in the United States Army, where he can be found in important post today.

The American Typewriter Company of New York also made in their factory at Bridgeport, Conn., a small machine listed at $5 to meet the demand for a child's writer, which enjoyed particular success during Christmas seasons. It was a flat machine printing from rubber type. Bernard Jensen, now head of the Arcade Typewriter Company in New York City, did much to create a large sale for this small American.

Annell

Model 4 of the Woodstock typewriter for a brief period in 1922 figured as the product of a mail order campaign conducted by the Annell Typewriter Company of Chicago. It bore the name of the Annell typewriter and for that reason is recorded here.

Archo

After three experimental models made their appearance, Model D Archo typewriter, manufactured by the Archo Typewriter Works of Winterling & Pfahl, Frankfurt a. M., Germany, made its initial appearance in 1920. It is of forward thrust typebar construction along the lines of the older Empire, has double shift and three rows of keys. It has many of the modern requirements embodied in its construction.

Arlington

R. W. Uhlig, who has invented a number of different writing machines on a variety of principles, devised a machine of this name which was so designated because of the place in which he lived at the time, Arlington, N. J. It was devised chiefly for overseas markets, was simple in construction, had double shift with keyboard of 29 keys and 87 characters and occupied a space of 12 in. x 12 in. x 6 in., weighing 14 lbs.

Armstrong

A machine of this name made considerable advancement under the guidance of a Mr. Bassett. It was manufactured and marketed by the British Typewriter Co., 193-195, Oxford Street, London, W., the factory being later located at Birmingham, England. It sold at a retail price of £19.15.0. The British Typewriter Company was a department of Ecco Works, Redditch, famous all over Europe for other goods. The product was the same as the typebar machine made and sold in the United States as the American.

Atlas

The Atlas Typewriter Company, 299 Broadway, New York City, was incorporated at $100,000 in January, 1915, to manufacture the Atlas typewriter for retail at $50. The machine had a double shift, occupied about a square foot of space and weighed about 15 lbs. The outstanding recommendations of the inventor were the small number of parts and ready adaptation to all languages. This was another of the several inventions of Richard W. Uhlig. Small quantities of machines were made but with the coming of the big war the manufacturing company was voluntarily disbanded.

Atlantia

The machine of this name is practically the same as the Commercial typewriter of Karl R. Kührt mentioned hereafter in this alphabetically arranged classification. The parts for the Atlantia typewriter, which dates from 1921, are manufactured in the factory of the gentleman named at Nürnberg, Germany, and assembled by the Atlantia Schreibmaschinenfabrik Bauereiss & Leisermann, of the same city, who also merchandise the machine. In Leipzig it is sold as the Arpha and some export trade has been carried on under the designation of Mepas.

Automatic

There will be readers who will recall the Automatic typewriter. Although a great deal was done the effort expended was quietly exerted. For a while it seemed to those close to the undertaking that there was in store for the machine a prosperous future, for it was not only brought to the model stage but was completely tooled, manufactured and presented to the public. Internal company troubles, however, brought its career to a close in 1883 after two years of considerable activity.

The Automatic typewriter was the invention of Major E. M. Hamilton, a resident of Brooklyn, N. Y., and an officer in the U. S. army. The machine is claimed by several to have been the first and original effort to produce a portable typewriter. It is furthermore claimed to have been one of the smallest practical typewriters ever made, excluding, of course, the stylus type of machines. The Automatic appeared before the days of aluminum, but even then weighed only about 11 pounds. It was of single shift with 48 keys and had typebars 1½ inches long. The Automatic, of course, was of the non-visible family, the writing being accomplished from an understroke against the platen, which was lifted to inspect the impressions. This machine has been often referred to as the Hamilton.

Avisso

The firm of Otto Schefter, Berlin, Germany, brought out during the current year the machine mentioned in the heading as a typewriter in size between the large standard and small portable machines. The Avisso shifts the segment, has 42 keys, single shift, ball-bearing carriage, two-color ribbon, back spacer, etc.

Barlock

In April, 1914, the Barlock Typewriter Company, Ltd., with chief offices in London and headed by the same interests then 23 years old as agents in distribution of the machine made in America, purchased from the Columbia Typewriter Manufacturing Company of New York all patents, registered name and all other rights, tools and machinery for manufacture of the Barlock typewriter. There had been some assembling of machines from parts

THE PRESENT No. 16 BARLOCK

shipped from America, but upon removal of the machinery to England in 1918 and establishment of a plant at Nottingham, complete and actual manufacture of the Barlock as a British product began. It also marked a notable instance of development from typewriter dealer to typewriter manufacturer, W. J. Richardson having headed the distributing company as he has also since been managing director of the manufacturing enterprise established in 1914.

A new model designated as No. 16 and differing entirely from anything previously known as Barlock typewriters was put on the market in May, 1921, by the Barlock Typewriter Co., Ltd., and stands as the current product of that British manufacturer. It has a single shift keyboard, 90 characters, is of unit construction and includes features in modern demand.

The No. 16 Barlock is the first standard All-British single keyboard typewriter ever produced. As will be seen from the illustration, it is a front strike segment machine. In appearance it is distinctive, especially in relation to the base of the machine, which is a one-piece casting closed in except for the space occupied by the typebars and keys. Thus the sound is shut in and the dirt kept out.

This closed in one-piece base casting was designed in conjunction with the unit system of construction. Like the modern motor car, each section is built as a unit complete in itself; manufactured, assembled inspected and tested as a separate unit.

The paper carriage is not only a unit complete in itself but constitutes a new and striking invention in typewriter construction. Instead of the spacing mechanism and motive power being part of the base with the latter transmitted to the paper carriage by a steel or leather band, the motive power is on the carriage itself, claimed to decrease lost motion and increase speed.

The paper carriages are made in four lengths, from 11 inches to 28 inches, and are all instantly interchangeable upon the one standard size base. All working parts, such as the paper carriage, tabulator stops and margin stops, are run on frictionless ball bearings.

In addition to the usual advantages of a standard machine, the new Barlock is fitted with a denominating tabulator, and can be used in combination with the four-column selector keys, permitting typing in 40 different positions on the ordinary 11-inch carriage, 80 positions on the 18-inch, and 106 positions on the 28-inch.

The keyboard is a single shift, with 45 keys printing 90 characters. The paper carriage is rigid, the typebar segment being operated by the shift key.

The No. 16 Barlock was designed in England by H. Etheridge, one of the Barlock staff, and the factory was laid out and organized under the management of Donald S. Richardson, the eldest son of W. J. Richardson, chairman and managing director of The Barlock Typewriting Company, Ltd., of London.

Baka

Manufacture Francaise des Cycles & Armes, St. Entienne, France, distributed the Moya typewriter, forerunner of the English Imperial, as the Baka 1 in France. This was in 1908. Following this experience in the marketing of writing machines the same house took up distribution of the Stoewer typewriter in France as the Baka 5. Neither venture materialized successfully.

Bamberger

A ribbon machine of this name made to sell at the equivalent of $17.50 in present-day value of American money was manufactured by Justin Wm. Bamberger & Company, 9 Menhauserstrasse, Munich, Germany.

Bavaria

Weighing a little less than 10 pounds, the Bavaria typewriter is a product of the works of Siegel Brothers, Altötting, Germany. It appeared on the market in 1921 and is designed to fill the need for a machine between the standard class and that of the smaller portable. It contains all requirements for mechanical writing, having double shift, 90 characters, front strike typebar and is furnished to buyers in its own traveling case.

Barratt

The Barratt Typewriter Company, 22, Cheapside, London, E. C., was mentioned in April, 1915, as prospective makers of writing machines and the product described. The machine was of standard type, front stroke design patterned after a German machine sold

in England before the outbreak of war. The project, which was said to have been backed in some manner by the British Government, did not go much beyond the preliminary announcement.

Bennett

This little machine was marketed first in 1910 by the Bennett Typewriter Company, Harrisburg, Pa., selling in the United States at a retail price of $18. It was manufactured in the factory of the Elliott-Fisher Company in the city named and was understood to be controlled by some interests affiliated with E-F, Geo. F. Watt being president of the company at one time.

Bennington

A machine of 68 keys with lower case and capitals from single shift, 26 of its keys each devoted in small letters to short and commonly used words or syllables, such as "the," "has," "be," etc. This machine was invented by W. H. Bennington, of Kansas City, Mo., in 1903, his ambition to put his idea on the market still being commendably alive; in a machine called the Xcel, recently described in these columns, Mr. Bennington has revived his undertaking.

The first printed mention of this syllabic or word writing machine is found in the October, 1905, issue of "Topics," where the sale in probate court at Dayton, Ohio, of the property of the Bennington Typewriter Company was confirmed. An effort made to start a factory in Dayton some years previous failed.

Blake

The Blake Typewriter Company, Newark, N. J., was incorporated in 1905 with capital stock of $1,000,000, C. Waldon Blake, formerly of the Manhattan typewriter enterprise, being one of the incorporators. The product was the former Manhattan typewriter which this later organized company acquired and planned again to manufacture. Sealed bids for the property of the Blake Typewriter Company were opened on June 25, 1909, by Thos. L. Raymond, receiver, at 164 Market St., Newark, N. J.

Blickensderfer

George C. Blickensderfer, whose name goes down in typewriter history as memorable, invented a small portable typewriter bearing his name. It employed a type-wheel for impression, was a

practical machine of proven durability and was sold and used in all countries of the world. Mr. Blickensderfer was born in Erie, Pa., but it was at Stamford, Conn., that he formed the Blickensderfer Manufacturing Company in 1889. The first machines came from the factory established at the same place in 1893, the first really practical lightweight typewriter produced in quantity. Like the Hammond, the initial machines had the Ideal keyboard, but to meet popular demand later changed to the Universal. The "Blick," by which name the machines almost through their entire life were known, printed direct from an ink roll; it had a double shift with keyboard of 28 keys and writing 84 characters. A hundred different keyboards were available through that many different type-wheels, accounting in part for the Blickensderfer popularity in so many countries. The writing was practically all visible. The machine was sold in France and some other countries as the Dactyle.

An improved model, No. 7, appeared in 1897, followed by another in 1905. The Blickensderfer was the first machine to be supplied in traveling bags for portability, a contribution of in-

terest to the traveling public being a machine with aluminum frame which saved weight. Model 8 appeared in March, 1908. There was also an electric machine which formed an important invention of Mr. Blickensderfer, this being utilized by the Telegraphic Mail Company of which much was heard at the time of its introduction. A music typewriter was also devised with the "Blick" as a basis in its construction. A standard $100 machine was also made.

On August 15, 1917, George C. Blickensderfer died and he was succeeded by Stephen S. Mapes as president of the company. The name was changed to the Blick Typewriter Company and in December, 1919, a typebar machine was brought out for sale at the same price of the former type-wheel machine, which was called the Blick Ninety. This, however, was the invention of L. R. Roberts; the late Mr. Blickensderfer's invention was practically discarded at this time. This latter mentioned fact was and still is, we might say here, the reason for much regret on the part of those who knew George C. Blickensderfer best, for his memory deserved perpetuation more in keeping with his contributions to the typewriter industry and his personal characteristics.

THIS ILLUSTRATES THE TYPEBAR PORTABLE, CALLED BLICK NINETY BECAUSE OF HAVING 90 CHARACTERS, WHICH APPEARED IN DECEMBER, 1919.

During the war the Blick factory at Stamford busily operated at substantial profit in manufacture of machine gun parts and a gun carriage which Mr. Blickensderfer invented. But everybody in the industry historically reviewed here remember him best as the inventor and maker of the first portable typewriter.

Blick-Bar

This machine, a product of outside purchase but manufacture by the Blickensderfer Mfg. Co., at Stamford, Conn., was the vehicle by which George C. Blickensderfer launched into the standard, front stroke field. It was the result of ten years' experiment when in December, 1913, this company began its manufacture. It was of simple construction, ball bearings were used on typebars, carriage, etc., and it possessed all points of modern demand. The war delayed delivery of machines as originally

planned, but in 1916 it was going strong and making a place for itself in the broadened field. The historian writing this paragraph firmly believes that if George C. Blickensderfer had lived the Blick-Bar would today be a big factor in the industry, but his death in 1917 threw the undertaking into complete discord and much money was lost through its unprofitable disposition to other interests. This standard typewriter was the invention of Emmet G. Latta, at the time and now located at Syracuse, N. Y., and backed by Harvey A. Moyer of the same city. The initial models were called the Moyer. After disposition by the Blickensderfer Mfg. Co., the same machine became the Harry A. Smith typewriter.

Book Electric

The invention of a telegraphic typewriter by S. T. Clevenger was taken over by the Book Electric Typewriter Co. which incorporated in Delaware in 1906 to build and market that machine.

Bradford

The Electric Power Typewriter Company, Bradford, Canada, was incorporated in 1906 to manufacture an electrically operated writing machine, which the patentee said would relegate then present styles to the junk pile. Among other things, a very enthusiastic correspondent wrote to this trade paper as follows:

"The gain in ease of operation is wonderful, but the most notable feature of the machine is remarkable increase in speed. In this new invention an ordinary operator can write nearly three times as fast as a first-class operator on the old style machines.

"Ordinary typewriters now have 70 or 80 characters, while on the new machine, owing to the fact the keys have only to be touched and not pressed down, there are more than three hundred different characters, including all the usual combinations of two or three letters and many of the small words in common use. To touch two keys at the same time instantly locks the machine and no impression is made. The instrument is what Edison calls 'fool proof,' and cannot get out of order, and especial care has been taken to make it durable. It will outlast two of the machines now in use and guaranteed for twenty years, except as to the wearing out of the face of the key. The cost of the machine will be $600, including the motor battery, which is good for one year."

Boston

This is the name assumed by the manufacturers of the World typewriter when introducing their machine into Europe, especially Germany. The project appears in history under the year 1888 and the machine was not dissimilar to the later American with which some of our readers are familiar.

Brooks

A machine of this name coming out in 1887 was famous for its few parts and light weight. It was invented by Byron A. Brooks and manufactured for the United Typewriter & Supplies

Company of New York, who controlled the marketing of it. Many of these machines were sold because of the visibility of the writing as the paper passed through the platen; the bars were arranged in a semi-circle behind the platen, as in the Fitch, three type to each bar and a double shift keyboard. The ribbon was controlled at the printing point by a pivoted vibrator which automatically raised to expose the print between type impressions. This vibrator also carried the ribbon forward and backward during the printing operation, to cause the entire surface of a wide ribbon to be brought to the printing point. The ribbon was only fed longitudinally by mechanism connected to the space key.

Burlingame

The United States Wireless Printing Telegraph Co., Canal-Louisianna Bank Bldg., New Orleans, La., were reported in May, 1908, as ready to start making machines invented by an Anderson, Ind., man of the same name as in the heading. The contrivance was for telegraphic transmission of print from one machine to another.

Caligraph

The Caligraph was the first commercial type-bar machine that was sold with a key for each character that it printed. It was put on the market about 1883 and was sold in large numbers.

The Model No. 1 printed only in upper case Gothic and Models Nos. 2, 3 and 4 printed both upper and lower case. It was an exceedingly simple machine mechanically and was very durable.

George Washington Yost, who had been actively identified with the Remington from the time it was first taken up by E. Remington & Sons, organized the Caligraph Patent Company in 1880 and with the co-operation of Franz Xavier Wagner worked out the Caligraph typewriter. He organized the American Writing Machine Company of New York to produce the machine, the factory being later moved to Bridgeport, Conn., where it remained for many years. The original Caligraph was similar to the early Remington with several refinements of its own. It was also called the New Century Caligraph, as was the visible writing Caligraph No. 10 called the Century. It was likewise made in Germany as the original Frister & Rossman typewriter.

Cardinal

A product of the current year is the Cardinal typewriter, a machine of standard size with 42 keys, front stroke and single shift. The segment on the Cardinal is shifted for capital writing, the bars are ball-bearing and the action easy. The machine is manufactured in three basic units and assembled separately, having the various requisite features demanded in modern construction and giving promise of creating a place for itself in the typewriter world. Although originally scheduled for manufacture in the Excelsior bicycle factory it is being produced in the watch and clock factory of L. Furtwängler & Sons A-G, Furtwangen, Baden, Germany.

Carmen

Originating in the year 1920, the Carmen typewriter belongs in the class of smaller machines half way between the standard and portable size. It has a double shift, 30 keys, front stroke action, two-color ribbon, interchangable carriage, automatic ribbon reverse and the various other requirements of a successful machine. It is produced and marketed by the Carmenwerke A. G., Stuttgart, Germany, and was originated by Carl Pistorius of Heidelberg.

Cash

A typewriter of this name was invented and first marketed in 1887 by Arthur Wise Cash of Hartford, Conn. Later models of this machine were known as the Typograph. It was a ribbon-writing, four-bank keyboard typewriter which instead of utilizing

a platen contained a flat paper carrier. The typebars stood erect in their normal position, alongside of each other in a sort of semi-circular arc, striking downward as operated.

Cartograph Tessari

Among the typewriters on display at the Office Equipment Exhibition in Venice in 1907 was the Cartograph Tessari.

Celtic

This is a French product designed by M. Gillant, an experienced typewriter engineer, in collaboration with M. Devliminck. They started work on the machine in 1913, but were prevented in

THE STANDARD CELTIC

complete development of it at the time due to the interruption of war. The first model was made in Lille, France, the Société des Moteurs Salmson of Billancourt, Paris, furnishing facilities in their automobile and aeroplane factory for resumption of experimental work in 1919. On June 10, 1920, the first machine was finished and the Celtic Corporation, 68 Rue Pierre Charon, Paris, was organized to make it. M. Alban Laibe was chosen as president of the manufacturing company, while a subsidiary was formed under the name of S. A. Celtic to handle the marketing of the machine.

The Celtic is built in five interchangable units, has universal keyboard of single shift giving 86 characters, interchangable carriages in six lengths, type basket shift, ball-bearing typebar pivot, uniform depression of keys, extra rapid escapement either single or double between characters, etc. All operations are from the keyboard and the machine possesses other features of its own and standard acceptance; and it is financed adequately by an impressive group of prominent Frenchmen who promise to give it a correspondingly important place in the minds of buyers of writing instruments of high grade.

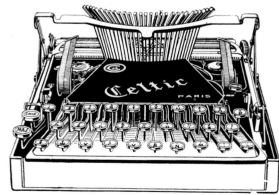

THE PORTABLE CELTIC

At the Foire de Paris in May last, the makers of the Celtic standard machine displayed for the first time a model of a portable typewriter which is capable of being folded up into small space and carried in an attaché case. It weighs about 2 kilos. 500, has 96 characters, three banks of keys with two shifts and has a depth of only 38 millimeters when folded. Future plans of Société Anonyme Celtic also embrace the bringing out of a bookkeeping machine and a noiseless typewriter.

Cereseto

In a typewriter show organized by Count Emilio Buslau as a part of an exhibition held under the auspices of the Building Art Society of Venice in 1907, an Italian typewriter called Cereseto was shown for the first and only time. The same exhibition included a number of shorthand and music-writing machines, but space does not permit any attempt in this story to cover the many inventions along those lines.

Champion

This was a machine which wrote all capital letters from a type-wheel through a ribbon. The Champion was made to sell at a low price, but it disappeared completely shortly after its inception in 1891.

Century

Small, compact and visible writing, this little machine was offered by the American Writing Machine Company in October, 1919, at a retail price of $60. It is a double shift machine taking

paper 9½ inches wide and writing a line 8 inches long and weighing 17½ lbs.

Probably the most interesting phase of the appearance of the Century from a historical standpoint was the return thereby of the American Writing Machine Company to a place among typewriter manufacturers, that company having years before been the makers of the old Caligraph and the New Century. Though the product in this case was not exactly new from an inventive angle, the Century No. 10 has its place in this narrative. It was manufactured in the Smith Premier factory at Syracuse, N. Y.

Champignon

A low priced typewriter of this name came out in 1898. It was an American product of the indicator type used so much in the effort to furnish something cheap, employed a type wheel and an ink roll in its construction.

Chicago

This was a wheel machine formerly known as the Munson. The aluminum Chicago at $50 was claimed by the makers to be the only typewriter with steel type which were instantly interchangable from one language to another. It had 48 styles of type to select from and even the key tops were interchangable. Two-color ribbon, patented eraser plate, envelope addressing plate for rapid work of this kind were features emphasized by the makers.

When this aluminum model of the Chicago was put out in 1915, great stress was put upon the 25 years which the machine had then been on the market.

The Galesburg Writing Machine Company, Galesburg, Illinois, were the manufacturers of this machine. An introductory scheme which took well in finding selling agents was to offer three (3) machines at $100, charges paid to destination and orders to be received within a specified time.

The same typewriter was last known as the Galesburg, but to the end manufactured by the Galesburg Writing Machine Co., with which for many years Harry A. Bates was prominently identified in executive capacity.

Childress

A secret code writing machine was invented and patented in June, 1922, by H. P. Childress, of Memphis, Tenn.

Cipher

This was a machine for the character of work indicated by its name, the invention of Frederick Sedgwick in October, 1916. The company organized for making and marketing was the International Cipher Writing Machine Company, 709 Reaper Block, Chicago, Ill.

The Hammond was used as a basis for the special equipment. It is said that the United States government used several Cipher machines, especially built, for secret code communication.

Chinese

A machine writing 4,200 characters and with only three keys, one of which was a back spacer and another the space key, was invented by Heuen Chi in May, 1915. He was a student inventor located at the time at 419 West 115th Street, New York City, and was said to have devised the first attempt at construction of a Chinese typewriter.

Cito

A 30-key, 90-character machine called the Cito appeared in 1904 and was retailed at 320 Marks by Bial & Greund, of Breslau II, in Germany and Austria, for whom it was manufactured by Bernh. Stoewer in practical duplication of the regular Stoewer typewriter made at that time.

Clevenger

Dr. S. C. Clevenger incorporated a company with capitalization of $100,000 at New Castle, Delaware, to manufcture a $10 typewriter of his invention, but it never appeared on the market.

Columbia

In 1883, at a time when the Remington and the Caligraph were the only typebar machines on the market, Charles Spiro began typewriter work in a little shop on Center Street in New York City.

He was interested in typebar machines principally, but while developing his plans for an improved standard typewriter, he designed and manufactured a small machine without keys and operated by one hand. This was the first machine with visible writing placed on the market. Its type was on the periphery of a wheel, which was twirled, with reference to an index plate, and an imprint made by depressing the wheel to the platen. The wheel automatically rose after the imprint and disclosed the writing. This was the machine known as the Columbia and had a considerable sale, being manufactured by the Columbia Typewriter Manufacturing Company who later turned out the better known Bar-Lock typewriter. The Columbia had an automatic inking device and variable spacing. The type wheels were interchangeable, so that different styles of type could be used. The patent covering this early invention of Mr. Spiro was dated June 28, 1885. He is one of the very few early typewriter inventors still living and it is the especial pleasure of the writer of this condensed history to thus publicly present the compliments of the entire industry to this veteran. Charles Spiro is deserving of much credit for the prominent part he has played in development of the writing machine and the opportunity he thereby helped to create for the many other office appliances whose existence are today directly accessory to and dependent upon the typewriter.

Columbia Bar-Lock

The initial appearance of a typewriter of this name was in 1888, the invention of the well known and versatile Charles Spiro, who also was responsible for the older Columbia typewriter.

The Columbia Bar-Lock was made by the same Columbia Typewriter Manufacturing Company, of New York, this machine having a key for every character. The American model had 78 keys and the one for European distribution 86 keys. In England, use by Royalty justified the prefix which was responsible for its being known there as the Royal Bar-Lock.

THE DOUBLE KEYBOARD COLUMBIA BAR-LOCK

It is claimed that the Bar-Lock was the first machine employing a hard rubber composition for keys, and, indeed, to Mr. Spiro is due the distinction of having blazed the trail in more than one instance. From the infancy of the industry he recognized the fact that only a keyed typewriter was suitable for commercial work, and so bent his efforts to the production of such a machine. Patents were issued under dates of April 2, 1889, September 2, 1890, and March 3, 1891, covering the features of the Columbia Bar-Lock, claimed to be the first keyed visible writer placed on the market. Its typebars stood upright and were pulled down to the platen to imprint. The basket containing the typebars was below the line of vision unless the operator sat far back, so later on the machine was provided with an inclined typebar basket. For several years it stood alone in the visible writing field.

Initial employment of wide typebar bearings as in the Columbia Bar-Lock is also credited to Mr. Spiro, covered by patents on March 7, 1899, and August 22, 1899. Acknowledging the lesson taught if two keys were depressed at the same time, Mr. Spiro provided the Columbia and Royal Bar-Lock with resilient typebars with a typebar lock as shown in his patent of March 26, 1889. A typewriter without a vibrating ribbon carrier would not be a visible writer, so, to complete his plan of visible writing, Mr. Spiro provided it, the first devised being described in patents dated May 25, 1892, and January 27, 1891. He also devised an automatic ribbon reverse and removable spools, patents dating from 1890 to 1899. The first practical tabulator was a feature of the Columbia Bar-Lock starting with the No. 4 under patents issued on July 23, 1895, and the interchangeable platen was first used in 1892. This was followed by the interchangeable carriages and on September 2, 1902, patents were issued covering the shift-key Bar-Lock as it first appeared.

Several different and improved models were brought out, including the No. 12 in 1907, another in 1908 and Model 14 in 1910. None of these machines in any manner resembled or had any connection with the Bar-Lock manufactured in England today by the Bar-Lock Typewriter Company at Nottingham. The sale in England and several continental countries of the former Bar-Lock was handled in the capacity of distributor by W. J. Richardson, now head of the British manufacturing enterprise continuing the same name.

THE SHIFT KEY COLUMBIA BAR-LOCK

Commercial (German)

In 1914 a machine of a little lower than standard price, with single shift, 86 characters and called the Commercial, was invented by Karl R. Kührt of Nürnberg, Germany, and it is being produced by the Commercial Schreibmaschinenfabrik Karl R. Kührt of the same city. The Commercial has an interchangeable type basket which adapts it to multi-language writing, in which respect it has been fairly successful. In other ways it has most of the usual modern refinements. The Commercial typewriter has also been sold as the Universal, Heros, Constanta, etc. For a short period this machine was sold as the Berolina.

Commercial Visible

In 1898, which was a particularly prolific year in contributions to typewriter history, a universal keyboard, 28-key, double-shift typewriter called the Commercial Visible made its bow. It em-

ployed a type wheel which, like most machines of that class, produced exceptionally clear and legible work. It was a visible writer, as the name implies, and the type wheels were interchangable. It had ten different spacings between lines, adjustment to which was easily done. The manufacturers were the Commercial Visible Typewriter Company, of New York, headed by Alexander M. Fiske, a man who is still actively attached to the writing machine in the capacity of exporter of all makes. R. W. Uhlig was the inventor of this machine, understood to have been the original of his many conceptions; it had but 288 parts and was one of the simplest writing machines ever devised.

Conqueror

Work on a writing machine was commenced in England as a post-war development by the Conqueror Typewriter Company, Limited, having as one of its prominent financiers Lord Lascelles, son-in-law of the King of England. A great deal of money was expended by the company, some of it impractically, but the Conqueror never saw the light of day. It was abandoned with finality in 1922. The Conqueror was intended to be the same as the pre-war Swift typewriter, better known to the international industry as the Stoewer.

Contin

This is one of the late additions to the writing machine industry provided by the recent entry of French manufacturers into this field. The title is an abbreviation of the company name, Etabliss-

ments Continsouza, whose head offices are located at 9 Rue du Commandant Rivière, Paris, France. They are makers of cinematograph machines universally used and the Director of Administration in the typewriter venture is Monsieur C. H. de Hainault, who entered the writing machine business in 1897 through taking the Oliver agency in France.

The Contin is standard in construction, having an interchangeable platen, removable carriage, inbuilt tabulator, single shift, writing 92 characters, a typebar action of exceptional merit, quick action escapement, etc. The factory in Paris in which the machine is made is modernly and adequately equipped for maximum efficiency in manufacture. The Contin was first introduced to the trade in August, 1922.

The initial announcement to the typewriter trade by which detailed acquaintance was made with the new Contin typewriter appeared in the August, 1922, issue of this trade paper. There was shown, besides the machine itself, a glimpse of the inside and an exterior view of the factory in which the Contin is being manufactured. The various points in the machine were covered exhaustively and provision for making typewriters by the Continsouza company was given as reason for anticipating an annual output of from twenty-five to thirty thousand machines. A more extensive outline of the connection with the industry of M. de Hainault than space permits here was also a part of the same story.

Continental

From Wanderer Fahrradwerke, at Schönau, near Chemnitz, Germany, came the Continental typewriter in initial product in 1904, selling at retail in Marks of that day at 340. A machine with tabulator sold at a price of 400 Marks, then the equivalent of $100 in American value. A four-rack tabulator was attached as regular equipment in Feb., 1914, the business at that date having expanded to a degree  which was highly impressive, for then the company occupied a large factory extension which was started in 1913. In the year just named, Continental typewriter production had reached the grand total of 60,000 machines.

The Continental typewriter has for several years occupied a very prominent position among the leaders in manufacture of machines of standard acceptance in Germany. It is a visible writer the makers of which have always been particularly aggressive in European markets.

The Wanderer company dates back to 1884, motor cycles being one of the chief products in early days; their product in that line received the grand prize in Paris in 1900. Ordinary cycles and milling machines were also a product of Wanderer Works.

Corona

The original Corona was built under the name "Standard Folding Typewriter," by the Rose Typewriter Company of New York City, the first shop being in a small loft on West 26th Street.

Some of the very early history is covered in more or less detail under Standard Folding heading

Model 1, the first typewriter with an aluminum frame, was placed on the market in 1906. This machine had no ribbon vibrator; the capital shift key was on the left side of the keyboard, the figure shift on the right; the paper fingers and margin stops were in one and were adjusted by means of a thumb screw; the ribbon spools were completely enclosed in aluminum cups; the corner posts were of aluminum, with brass bushings and the folding arms and key levers were of aluminum.

In July, 1909, the Standard Typewriter Company was incorporated and took over the Rose Company. A few months later the plant was moved from New York City to its present location, in Groton, N. Y.

Model 2 was placed on the market in 1910. In this machine steel folding arms were introduced, in place of aluminum; both shift keys were placed on the left of the keyboard; a ribbon

vibrator was added; spring adjusted margin stops were employed and many other minor refinements made. This model, like No. 1, was finished in natural aluminum.

Model 3 came out in 1912, and with this model the name was changed to Corona; the finish was changed to black, the frame was widened at the keyboard, sheet metal ball races were introduced, a scale was added, a new type of all steel, one piece key lever was adopted and a seven-yard ribbon took the place of the five-yard ribbon used on Models 1 and 2.

The type bars on the earlier No. 3 Coronas were on individual hangers of the pivot style.

About a year and a half later, the pivot style of hanger was abandoned in favor of a ball-bearing hanger and in 1915 the solid segment was adopted.

In May, 1914, the name of the company was changed from Standard Typewriter Co. to Corona Typewriter Co., Inc.

In December, 1915, radical changes were made in the universal bar action and the escapement; improvements were also made in the spring drum, line spacer, ribbon vibrator and paper release; a line lock was added and the type rest was suspended on supports extending from the segment instead of the middle of the frame. This model was called "The Improved Corona."

In 1917, changes were made in the ribbon feed mechanism, in order to reduce the speed of the ribbon feed.

In an effort to comply with the wishes of the War Industries Board as to conservation of metal, a light type of folding arm was designed and adopted in 1919. Less than 50,000 machines were made with this type of arm.

The last radical change in Corona occurred in 1922 when the use of a model number was discontinued; the carriage was widened to ten inches; a combination line space and carriage return lever was added, an automatic ribbon reverse installed and the frame widened in front to allow for the addition of right-hand shift keys and a wider key spacing. Another new Corona was described in the last issue of this magazine.

THE "CORONA XC-D"

This new machine is called the "Corona XC-D." It has all of the improvements recently incorporated, notably ten-inch carriage, automatic ribbon reverse and right and left shift keys. It has two more keys than the standard Corona and is so designed that from one to four keys may be disconnected from the escapement mechanism, so that while they will write they will not move the carriage.

Dead keys are a very important feature of a typewriter employed in writing a language which requires accented letters, but it is hardly practicable to employ dead keys unless the typewriter is equipped with more than the usual eighty-four characters.

While this ninety character Corona was undoubtedly designed primarily to meet the demand of the export field, it is also being put out in the American market for the use of engineers, chemists and others whose work requires the employment of special symbols and characters. For such use the machine is furnished without dead keys.

It is understood that later in the year the Corona Company will further enlarge its field by the introduction of a reverse carriage model, for languages like Turkish, Yiddish and Arabic, which read from right to left.

From Model No. 1 to the present machine the retail price (in U. S. A.) has always been $50.

Courier

The Courier typewriter was a creation of the year 1903 and was manufactured by A. Greger & Company, of Vienna, Austria, makers also of the Courier bicycle. It was the first writing machine to be manufactured in Austria, and although completely produced in Vienna was a very close adaptation of the Oliver No. 3.

Cram

The Cram Writing Machine Company opened offices at 220 Broadway, New York City, in September, 1907, for sale of a combination writing and adding machine called the Cram. Little progress was made by the undertaking.

Crandall

If an effort were made to inflate the numerical presentation of typewriters in this historical treatment, this subject could be divided to embrace more than one machine of quite different nature which sold under the name of Crandall. In 1879 Lucien Stephen Crandall invented the first which was manufactured by the Crandall Machine Company at Groton, N. Y. It is said that C. Latham Sholes and James Densmore were also interested in this venture, which entailed the production of a machine which wrote from an upright sleeve construction cylindrical type-wheel of hard rubber having six characters in each vertical row. The keyboard was arranged in three rows, spacing being done by means of a key in the center. Each key represented capitals, lower case and figure characters. The illustration is shown through kindness of the Royal Typewriter Co.

The Universal Crandall was the third model of the Crandall machines, this being a double shift, keyboard typewriter writing from a type cylinder. It was a considerable improvement over earlier models and while similar to its predecessor carried throughout its life the distinguishing prefix "Universal" as a mark of difference from the first Crandall typewriter. Its retail price was $75.

The Improved Crandall of 1895 by the same inventor was a sort of type-bar machine of novel action. Printing was from an ink roll. Upon the depression of a key the correct type was thrust forward which secured its ink from the roll when passing. This type "tongue" had insufficient power behind it to do its own printing, but simultaneously with the stroke an overhead hammer struck downward upon the type from above. This was a 36-key, 72-character machine. The last model was brought out with a ribbon mechanism for two colors. The maker of this machine was the Crandall Typewriter Company with a factory in Chicago, Ill.

From 1877 to 1899, E. E. Barney, since 1918 at the New York office in general charge of development work for the Remington Typewriter Co., was with the Crandall Typewriter Company at Groton, N. Y., as superintendent of the factory from 1891 to 1899

Crown

A complicated mechanism brought out by the Crown Typewriter Manufacturing Company of Albany, N. Y., in 1887. Its operating and printing mechanism was enclosed in a circular shaped box, the typebars standing upright and striking down onto the platen below. The typebars were peculiarly shaped. The keyboard was arranged in a circle on top of the enclosing box and while requiring some training to operate was rather slow. Very interesting is the fact that a word counter was built into the Crown, the first and only ever to contain such a device integrally. It retailed at $20.

Crown of 1894

Here we are obliged to separate the narratives of typewriters known as the Crown, for the combination indicator and type-wheel machine invented by Byron A. Brooks in 1894 had no connection with the entirely different type of machine which is described as an offering of the year 1887. The later machine named Crown was manufactured by the National Meter Company of New York City and resembled the Peoples typewriter. By coincidence, Byron A. Brooks patented his Brooks typewriter in 1887, the same year in which the first machine named Crown appeared in Albany.

Culema

A front stroke typebar machine of double shift, 30 keys, and with the usually required features is briefly descriptive of the Culema typewriter which made its initial appearance in 1920. Model 4 is the machine at present being made, distinctive in the probable fact that it is the only machine that is contained within its own housing at all sides and top and bottom. The Culema is the product of Lehmann Bros., of Erfuhrt, Germany.

Dactygam

A small, portable affair with 5 keys and worked by one hand. By use of combinations of the 5 keys, it was possible to print 30 characters. The Dactygam typewriter was made up of only 120 parts. Inventor: M. Georges Maulin, Mortain-Manache, France.

Darling

A product of 1910 and a so-called pocket typewriter was the Darling marketed by the Ingersoll watch interests of New York. It was an extremely small machine which used a small revolving dial for indication of the letters to be written, printing only capitals from a type wheel and ink roll. The Darling retailed at a very low price, having its largest demand as a toy. In several European countries it was also sold as the Trebla.

Daugherty

This machine was among the first completely visible writing, single shift typewriters brought onto the market. It had the

Above is a picture of tne later and better known Crandall typewriter. The larger illustration at the left, printed by courtesy of the Royal Typewriter Co., shows the L. S. Crandall writing machine of 1881, photographed by permission of the Smithsonian Institute, Washington, D. C., where it is exhibited in the National Museum as No. 251,217.

regular four rows of keys, the typebars lay in a flat position when at rest and struck forward upon the platen, describing the usual movement of front stroke machines. Although there were other previously issued patents on typebar actions like that used on the Daugherty, including the well-known invention of W. H. Slocum of Buffalo, the machine here described was earlier in the use of such construction through actual manufacture. It was a completely visible writing machine without obstructions of any nature. The Daugherty was introduced in 1890, the invention of James D. Daugherty, a former stenographer, and was manufactured by the Daugherty Typewriter Company of Kittaning, Pa., It sold, with a cover, for $75.

The first Daugherty typewriters were manufactured in the plant of the Crandall Typewriter Company at Groton, N. Y., its initial production being intrusted to the supervision of the well-known E. E. Barney, who was superintendent of the Crandall plant at the time.

Dayton

A portable typewriter called the Dayton, designed with four rows of keys and single shift, front stroke, typebars and many other modern features, and scheduled to sell at a retail price of $35, is destined to appear officially on the market within the course of the next few months.

Dea

This typewriter is classed with the standard products and was first announced to the trade in January, 1909. Features emphasized by the manufacturer was no finger fatigue, practically noise-

less and special atachments in-built, "a first class German typewriter for dealers outside Germany." The maker was Akt.-Ges. vorm. Gustav Krebs, Typewriter Works, Halle-a.-S., Germany. The Dea was first called the Union typewriter, but the name heading the classification was taken later and the earlier title dropped in order to avoid confusion with other people already controlling the word "Union" as applied to a typewriter.

Delta

This was the name of one of the numerous machines invented by Richard W. Uhlig, who, throughout his long career as a deviser of writing instruments invented fifty complete machines. Twenty of them were developed to the model stage, and although long connected with this class of work is still more active than many much younger in years. He lives at present at 924 Turner St., Allentown, Pa., where he is at the time this is published working on a new typewriter to be called the Modern.

Demountable

There was organized under the laws of the State of New Jersey in the year 1911, the Harris Typewriter Company. It manufactured and sold the Harris three-bank typewriter in the United States. In 1914 the company reorganized under the name of the Rex Typewriter Company, manufacturing the Rex typewriter and disposing of its product throughout the world.

During May, 1916, the Rex Typewriter Company acquired the right to manufacture the National Portable typewriter, which had just been invented. This first model was the No. 2 and later the No. 3 and No. 5 were developed. This portable typewriter has been manufactured and sold ever since.

It was during October, 1918, that work was started on the de-

velopment of the standard, four-bank typewriter, now marketed under the name of the Demountable typewriter. This new typewriter was planned and later built by hand and it was not until during the early part of 1921 that the first model was completed and demonstrated. At that time the company commenced manufacturing this new Demountable typewriter. Demountable typewriters have since been manufactured in large quantities in the factory at Fond du Lac, Wis. The company is now amply financed for large production and distribution. It owns its own land, buildings, power plant and machinery, all of which are well adapted to typewriter manufacture.

During March, 1923, the company officially changed its name under the laws of the State of Wisconsin to the Demountable Typewriter Company. The name is now in keeping with the copyrighted name of the company's principal product, the Demountable typewriter.

The Demountable typewriter is now being sold throughout the United States and in all the principal foreign countries. The perfecting of this typewriter is more than a triumph of invention. With half a dozen simple movements and without the use of tools, the Demountable may be separated into its three basic units—frame, carriage and action unit. All of these units are absolutely interchangeable, so if the action unit from one typewriter, the frame from another and the carriage from a third were assembled, the complete typewriter would operate as efficiently as any of the three Demountables from which it was made. For cleaning or replacement, it is also possible to take out the paper table, platen, deflector plate and feed rolls.

The officers of the Demountable Typewriter Company are Wm. Mauthe, president and general manager; F. J. Reuping, vice-president; T. L. Doyle, secretary; H. R. Potter, treasurer, and G. B. Sherman and T. H. O'Brien, directors. G. T. Martin is the superintendent and E. R. Roll the mechanical engineer, with G. J. Reeh at the head of the sales department and C. J. Fay in charge of advertising. Mr. Sherman has taken over the Demountable sales organization for Chicago and surrounding territory with offices in the Monadnock Building, Chicago. The European sales director and the London representative for the British Isles have successfully established active sales agencies throughout the British Isles, France, Belgium, Norway, Holland, Sweden, Spain and Czecho-Slovakia. Aggressive sales agencies have also been established in Canada, Australia, New Zealand, Cuba, East Indies and China.

Diamont

A portable typewriter of 90 characters, double shift and three rows of keys is the Diamont which first appeared on the market in 1921. It has customary features and is furnished with a traveling case. The Diamont is the invention of Jacob Heil and is being manufactured and marketed by the Diamont Schreibmaschinen Fabrik, G.m.b.H., of Frankfurt, a. M., Germany. This machine is sold in England as the Diamond by the Guarantee & St. Martin's Wholesale Typewriter Co., Ltd.

Diskret

An improved model of the Volks typewriter manufactured by Fr. Rehmann, Karlsruh, Germany, was offered in 1899. It was called the Diskret and although much superior to the Volks, its lack of speed and other shortcomings resulted in it having but a brief sojourn in the typewriter race.

Densmore

The Densmore machine was put on the market in 1891, and was of the "understrike" variety. Its principle feature was the use of ball bearings for the pivoted type bars, and many other

parts. It is u n d erstood t o h a v e chiefly been the invention of Walter J. Barron, a relative o f James Densmore.

The selling end of the Densmore typewriter business was taken over in 1907 by the American Writing Machine Company,

with general offices then at 345-347 Broadway, New York City, but this representation was later relinquished and the machine gradually disappeared from the market. It was made in a variety of models and several men still prominent in the industry made their reputations through connection with the Densmore typewriter enterprise.

Dollar

The well-known manufacturers of dollar watches, Robert Ingersoll & Bros., New York City, brought out a series of so-called Dollar typewriters for the use of children, starting in 1903. Various models of the Ingersoll machines were known as the Baby Practical, Little Giant, Practical, Simplex, etc. They were all the indicator type of little printing device with rubber type. The Simplex is still being manufactured by the Simplex Typewriter Co., 210 11th Avenue, New York City, and enjoys an active holiday sale in toy and department stores.

Duplex

This was an unusual type of machine that provided for two keys being depressed at the same time; hence its name. By this action, of course, two characters were simultaneously printed in

a theoretical endeavor to increase speed. The Duplex, which dated from 1895, was of the key for every character type of machine and had the liberal number of 100 keys. The keyboard was not of universal arrangement, being not only peculiarly its own but very different from any other machine. Typebars were used and it had an automatic ribbon reverse. The machine never registered much success, though it was a wonder from a mechanical angle. It was made by the Duplex Typewriter Company of Des Moines,

Iowa, somehow connected with the Jewett undertaking of the same city. An older model was known as the Dennis-Duplex and was a pad-inking machine. This is the machine illustrated.

D. W. F.

A new universal keyboard typewriter named the "D. W. F." made its initial bow to the industry by announcement in the September number of this international magazine, thereby entailing by

narrow margin inclusion in this historical resumé of machines coming onto the market during the fifty years which this special issue seeks to tabulate. This latest of German machines entering the industry is manufactured by the Berlin Karlsruher Industrie Werke A-G., Berlin, and is distributed exclusively by Schaefer & Clauss, Leipzigerstr. 19, Berlin W. 8.

The D. W. F. has the forward thrust typebar action, of double shift, three rows of keys and contains thirty keys and ninety total characters. It has all the features included in modern writing machine construction, a light moving carriage, good manifolding power, and clear legible type. It is built of excellent materials, is durable and promises a lengthy stay on the typewriter market.

Edelmann

A low-priced typewriter belonging to the variety of the Hall, Graphic, etc., which overcame the previously developed shortcomings of such machines in their invisible writing and lack of manifolding power. The Edelmann employed a type-wheel for printing. Its keyboard could not really be called such, as it was arranged in two straight printed rows in front of the machine, before which was a notched scale into which the handle was inserted in location of the characters. The machine was gradually improved and later brought out with many modern features, the first one dating from 1897. A. Greef & Co., Frankfort a. M., were identified with the undertaking and although made by Wernicke, Edelmann & Co. of Berlin, the Edelmann is now in the hands of J. Pintsch A-G., of Frankfurt a. M., Germany.

Edland

Invented by Jos. E. Edland, of Brooklyn, in 1894 and produced by the Liberty Manufacturing Company of New York City. Two models were manufactured. After the fashion of the indicator type of machines, but more efficient and rapid, printing on the Edland was done by means of a three-row wheel with the keyboard arranged in front in a semicircle. Through means of grooves on the keyboard, the indicator could be moved to the desired place and instantaneously depressed for the accomplishment of writing.

Elliott-Fisher

Most men are naturally conservative.

A conservative man may be defined as one who is prone to hold upon an established idea and slow to accept a new one.

The struggles of every inventive genius have been quite as much occasioned by this natural conservative tendency as they have had to do with the financing of their projects.

Every mechanical device designed for the purpose of saving time and labor has had to go through this painful period of transition.

Many of the objections raised against mechanical innovations seemed very formidable at the time they were uttered, but seem to us quite ridiculous now, after their achievements have been demonstrated.

EARLY TYPE ELLIOTT-FISHER USED FOR BOUND BOOK RECORDS

In all the world's history the last fifty years have brought forth more phenomenal mechanical progress than any previous five hundred.

One cannot associate machines with man-power without unconsciously thinking what the machine has meant in the process of raising living standards.

Manifestly any attempt to enter into an exhaustive review of mechanical science would carry us into volumes of data.

Of every group of machines designed to do a certain type of work, there stands out one idea well to the forefront of all others.

A very striking illustration of this measure of perfection obtains in the writing machine.

The writing machine, or typewriter, was originally designed to overcome the handicaps of illegible chirography, and make the writing of more than one copy of a document possible.

Incidentally, the question of labor was one of some consideration, but the primary purpose behind the idea of the writing machine was legibility.

The typewriter of today is given over, almost exclusively, to the writing of correspondence, but out of the idea of writing readable characters with perfect registration and clearness has expanded the application of machine writing to the art of bookkeeping.

In the products manufactured by the Elliott-Fisher Company, of New York and Harrisburg, Pa., there is one of these notable outstanding features that make the Elliott-Fisher quite separate and apart from all other writing equipments.

Possibly in the strictest sense of the word, what are these days exclusively referred to as Elliott-Fisher accounting machines should not be regarded as typewriters, yet within the industry there has been no disassociation and this machine which in its inception was intended and patented for writing in bound books takes its place in this compilation.

The original idea of the inventor to find a mechanical principle which would enable him to write on a perfectly flat surface has been retained in the constant improvement of all Elliott-Fisher equipments.

A machine that will write on a piece of paper is one thing, but a machine that will write in a bound book without removing pages or on a heavy piece of cardboard without bending it, is quite another.

The introduction of the flat writing principle as embodied in the Elliott-Fisher became a commercial proposition of some proportions about a quarter of a century ago. Since the organization of the Elliott-Fisher Company, bringing together as it did a consolidation of genius, capital and patent rights, the perfection of the flat writing principle has gone ahead by leaps and bounds.

Today there is practically no business of any dimensions in any part of the commercial world that has not found in Elliott-Fisher a revelation in the matter of compiling permanent records of various types.

Robert L. Fisher, who was a cashier of the First National Bank of Athens, Tenn., invented the Fisher book typewriter in 1896. He took his first model to Cleveland, Ohio, to show to H. J. Halle and the Fisher Book Typewriter Company was formed soon after with Mr. Halle as president and general manager. In the development to the present E-F broadly serviceable machines in accounting work from the original device, which was made only for typewriting in bound books, the adding attachment became a feature in 1902. In March, 1903, the Fisher Book Typewriter Company consolidated with the Elliott-Hatch Book Typewriter Company, the American Railway, American Standard and Keystone company interests and the Elliott-Fisher Company came into existence. At that time the general offices were at 329 Broadway, New York City, and the factory at Harrisburg, Pa., where it is still located.

On May 1, 1908, the general offices were moved to the factory, but when M. S. Eylar, who started his career in the typewriter business in 1889 by selling Caligraphs on the road, became vice-president in charge of E-F sales, the headquarters were returned to New York, where, since May, 1921, they have been in the Canadian Pacific Building on Madison Avenue. Another important event in Elliott-Fisher history was the breaking of ground in November, 1912, for factory additions which greatly increased manufacturing facilities. The famous model "T" came out in February, 1914. Philip D. Wagoner returned to the presidency of the company in February, 1921, after previously heading the

PRESENT TYPE OF ELLIOTT-FISHER UNIVERSAL ACCOUNTING MACHINE

enterprise from August, 1918, to December, 1919. Another personality of prominence attached to Elliott-Fisher was the late George F. Watt, remembered almost solely through his association with that company.

The present prosperous Elliott-Fisher enterprise reflects monumentally upon its founders, the late United States Senators Grant B. Schley of New York and Cameron of Pennsylvania. A son of the former, K. B. Schley, member of the New York banking house of Moore & Schley, is chairman of the present board of directors. The Elliott-Fisher Company is the largest exclusive manufacturer of accounting-writing machines in the world. It has pioneered in this field and ever since the inception of the idea has stood for better and improved accounting equipment.

Emerson

Although the enterprise eventually developed into something markedly different both as to personnel and product, that fact in itself gives a place in this historical presentation exclusively to the Emerson

typewriter. The Emerson Typewriter Company was organized at Kittery, Me., in September, 1907, with authorized capital of $500,-000. H. Mitchell, of the same city, was president and the purpose was to manufacture the Emerson typewriter and to sell it at a retail price of $50. R. W. Uhlig, whose name appears itor.

The typebar action of the Emerson was novel. A rotary action, something like the Hammond, was here employed for the first time to typebars, which stood at rest in two divisions on either side and traveled by a side motion to the printing point.

The first marketing attempt was made from a Boston office located at 165-167 High St., with George M. A. Fecke as general manager. In 1908 the general offices were moved to Chicago and a plant was opened at Momence, Ill., where numbers of this ingeniously devised typewriter were turned out and sold. In 1910, Mr. Sears, one of the founders of the famous mail order house of Sears, Roebuck & Co. of Chicago, acquired the Emerson business. On April 21, 1910, shortly after the aforementioned change of hands, a big banquet was held in the factory building which was to and which has since housed this manufacturing and marketing enterprise, though now it is the Woodstock Typewriter Company well known to the entire industry. There was a change of name in between to the Roebuck Typewriter Company, when an entirely new front stroke typewriter was announced.

Empire

In 1892 Wellington P. Kidder invented the Empire typewriter and from 1895 on it was manufactured by the Williams Manufacturing Company for the Imperial Writing Machine Company of

No. 1 EMPIRE

Montreal, Canada. Dr. C. W. Colby, now president of the Noiseless Typewriter Co., headed the Imperial company for a considerable period and deserves extreme credit for the eventual world-wide popularity of the Empire. The initial product was a double shift visible writing machine of typebar construction. The straight forward thrust of the bar has figured prominently in the world-wide manufacture and marketing of mechanical writing devices, the typebar construction principle of

the Empire typewriter opening possibilities which have been broadly embraced.

The Empire was a complete success in Canada and the later models were satisfactorily exploited in all markets of the world. In the United States the machine was manufactured at Plattsburg, N. Y., by the Williams Mfg. Co. and called the Wellington.

In 1901 George H. Bland journeyed from Montreal to manage the British business and to open the office in London from which he developed a big business and a highly enviable reputation as a leader among typewriter men.

Several models, each an improvement, were made and the latest of the offerings still has a wholesome demand in many countries This includes a lightweight model of the Empire which came out in May, 1916, weighing 10½ lbs. Manufacture for German distribution was intrusted many years ago to Adler Fahrradwerke vorm. Heinrich Kleyer, Frankfort, Germany, who made a very satisfactory product that enjoyed a wide sale, but upon expiration of patents in 1912, the Canadian factory resumed direct deliveries to Germany, calling the machine the Davis.

To go back a little: The No. 2 Empire came out in 1908 and the No. 3, which embraced the addition of a right-hand capital shift, was placed on the market in 1921 as a product for sale only in Canada; the No. 2 remains as the machine marketed at export. Since then there has been little change in the product though this enterprise which has long produced the only Canadian typewriter is now known as the Empire Typewriter Company of Canada, Ltd., E. D. Twite being the managing director.

English

Manufactured by the English Typewriter Company of London, the invention in 1890 of Morgan Dunne and Michael Hearn, the English typewriter was a machine of more than passing merit. It was quite visible in writing and combined two good principles of its day in typewriter construction, and semi-circular arrangement of keyboard, like in the early Hammond and Crandall, and the upright, downward stroke typebars like the Bar-Lock. It wrote through a ribbon. The English was sold only in England, but never reached a very successful stage.

Erika

This is the name of the portable typewriter product made and sold by the well-known house of Seidel & Naumann A-G., of Dresden, Germany. It is also marketed in some localities as the Bijou.

Essex

The first Essex produced in 1890 had only 16 keys in two rows, but later models contained 27 keys writing 81 characters by use of the double shift. Its writing was originally done from an ink roll but later through a ribbon. The typebars stood upright in a segment and the print was partially visible. The Essex, manufactured by the Essex Universal Typewriter Compaany of New York, did not have a wide sale.

Eclipse

This was a typewriter of the ribbon writing variety which had come and gone in the year 1898.

Elliott-Hatch

Designed solely as a book typewriter, the Elliott-Hatch was a single shift-key machine, had the flat platen underneath the writing mechanism and was possessed of features valuable and serviceable in development of that branch of the writing machine industry which is today meeting the demand for bookkeeping machinery. Five models were made, differing only in capacity as to dimensions of pages upon which they would write. They ranged from one for pages 18½ inches long by 9 inches wide, selling at $175, to the No. 5 which wrote on an 18½ by 21-inch page and sold at $200. As recorded elsewhere, the Elliott-Hatch was combined with the Fisher and its features embodied into the Elliott-Fisher. Messrs. Elliott and Hatch are both still living, the former working on book typewriters in New York and the latter in France in connection with promotion of a small typewriter.

Ellis

Appearing first on the market in 1910, the Ellis, a complete adding and billing machine and, to considerable extent, an accounting machine, due in great part to its construction along orthodox typewriter lines, calls for mention in this history. The

Ellis is visible writing, has a typewriter as well as adding machine keyboard, contributing to its usefulness as an adding machine by combining the functions of a typewriter—e. g., its ability to write with a single stroke such words as debit, credit, etc. The more technical features of construction that concern the Ellis probably fit more correctly into a history of computing devices, but suffice it to say, in addition, that it is the product of the Ellis Adding Typewriter Company of Newark, N. J., and the invention of Halcolm Ellis, a gifted inventor who has since given us the M. A. P. typewriter of France.

Eureka

This machine was of the toy class. It utilized rubber type, flat printing and had a keyboard on a circular plate at the top of the machine. The Eureka was of American manufacture but was sold only in France.

Excelsior

As explained under the Franconia heading of this story, the latter machine, subsequently the Omega, appeared in greatly refined and improved form in 1921 as the Excelsior, the product of Mayer & Co., of Augsburg, Germany. The latter, officially operating as the Schreibmaschinenfabrik Augsburg, A-G., manufacture the present Excelsior machine and it is exclusively distributed by the Excelsior Maschinen G.m.b.H., of Berlin.

The Excelsior is a thoroughly standard and high-grade typewriter, front stroke, single shift, 86 characters and all the many characteristics which contribute to the essentials of the modern machine. During the current year, Model 2 Excelsior appeared in durable and attractive form and is already enjoying a strong and healthy sale. Model 2 has 90 characters, two-color ribbon and further appealing features.

Excelsior Script

The Excelsior Script and Typewriting Machine Company of San Francisco, Cal., introduced a machine which they claimed was the only one that would write either in script or ordinary type at any time without change in the machine. A proposed novelty was to supply type in exact facsimile of the purchaser's handwriting, guaranteeing perfect connection between all letters when written. Excelsior Script and Typewriting Machine No. 1 was listed at $75.

Faktotum

This machine appeared in 1912 as the product of Fabig & Barschel, Charlottenburg, Germany, and was manufactured by them for sale by the Apparate-Industrie A-G., of Germany. The Faktotum was almost identical with the original British Imperial, containing upright bars which struck downward, and sold at a very moderate price. With the dissolution of the Apparate-Industrie, the Fabig house took the distribution themselves and brought out Model 2 in 1914, discontinuing in 1916. The same machine was also sold as the Leframa & Forte-Type and is now being manufactured in improved form as the Rofa.

Famos

This can be included among the stylus class of machines. The Famos, invented by Gustave Tiesse, of Liepzig, Germany, made its appearance in 1910 and had an upright circular dial carrying the lettering which was revolved till the desired character had reached its printing point and impression made by pressure on a knob beneath. It retailed at a very low price and was sold in France as the Victoria.

Federal

In December, 1919, the Federal Adding Machine Company, of which J. B. de Beltrand was the president, acquired from the old Columbia Typewriter Mfg. Company, the Visigraph Type-

writer Company and the C. Spiro Mfg. Company all the interest in and equipment for making the latest typewriter invention of Charles Spiro. It was renamed the Federal and offered in conjunction with the adding machine product of the Federal company, broad plans for expansion announced soon after including the joining of E. J. Manning with the enterprise as second vice-president in charge of production. Later stories conveyed details of the sale of the typewriter end of the Federal business to the Hammond Typewriter Corporation.

As indicated in reference to the same machine when called the Visigraph it employed the knife blade typebar and segment construction so popular today; it had many distinctive and modern features, including a removable and interchangeable carriage through the manipulation of a small lever in the rear.

Felio

A machine of the name in the heading appeared first in Holland as the product of the N. V. Eerste Nederlandsche Schrijfmachine-Fabrik Felio, Lauriergracht 107, Amsterdam, the first institution to undertake the manufacture of a writing machine in that country. The Felio, of single shift, four rows of keys, 84 characters, front stroke typebar construction and flat in appearance, reminding one greatly of the No. 5 Royal, had a brief but interesting history.

The Felio company in Holland brought the machine out first in 1919, that company abandoning it in 1921. Its sale was continued in Holland by a previous manager of the company, but its production reverted back to Berlin, Germany, from whence it originally came.

The same machine as the Felio appeared first in 1914 as the Nora typewriter and was the invention of a Mr. Aron. It was the product first of the firm of Dreusicke & Galz, of Berlin, and later of the Nora Schreibmaschinen G.m.b.H., following which it was sold to the Holland interests. For a short time the Nora was sold in Berlin as the Berolina typewriter, but should not be confused with the Berolina that resembled the Commercial of Germany.

Ford

A machine with typebars operated by the forward thrust action, similar to the Empire and Rapid. It was a double shift machine with 27 keys writing 81 characters and wrote through a ribbon. The first machine appeared in 1895, an aluminum model being made later. The Ford was manufactured by the Ford Typewriter Company of New York, but, as has been recorded in a couple of instances, Henry Ford of automobile fame had nothing to do with it. This machine was introduced in France as the Hurtu and assembled and sold in Germany as the Knoch.

Franconia

A front-stroke, single-shift, 86-character machine of orthodox design and simple enough construction to warrant sale at a lower than standard prevailing price was the Franconia typewriter. It was invented by C. F. Kührt of Nürnberg, Germany, and manufactured for him by Otto Baldamus of Koburg, Germany, who undertook the making of it for himself in 1911 in improved form. Manufacture of the machine ceased with the beginning of the World War, but in 1919 the Franconia was rejuvenated through its acquisition by the firm of Mayer & Co. of Augsburg, Germany, who produced and sold it as the Omega. In 1921 the latter named greatly improved the product and called it the Excelsior.

Fitch

A small typebar machine and one of the earliest on which the writing was visible to the operator. It was invented by Eugene Fitch of Des Moines, Iowa. The Fitch was not unlike in key-

board the early Crandall and Hammond, having two rows of 26 keys in all and writing 78 characters through the use of two shift keys and three characters to the key. A later model had the keys arranged in three rows. The Fitch was patented in 1886.

Fay-Sholes

The story about the Remington-Sholes contains reference to the time when, as a result of litigation, the Remington-Sholes Typewriter Company was ordered by the Court to remove the name "Remington" from their title. In response to this compulsory demand, the name of "Fay" was substituted, C. N. Fay at the time being president of the company, and one of its prime movers.

It was while the enterprise was operating under the name of the Fay-Sholes Typewriter Company that the change mentioned elsewhere was made to the Arithmograph Company, the Arithmograph having been acquired and attached to the Fay-Sholes typewriter in manufacture of an adding typewriter. The accompanying illustration is reproduced herewith from an issue of this magazine in 1905.

A study of the billhead presenting an example of the work done on that combination adding machine and typewriter clearly shows how in the days here reviewed The Arithmograph Company was operating as the manufacturers of the Fay-Sholes typewriter and the Arithmograph. The illustration also provides excellent presentation of how the Fay-Sholes typewriter looked with the Arithmograph mechanism attached to it. Readers should be reminded that the Fay-Sholes typewriter was non-visible, as were also the early Remington-Sholes.

We very much wish that we might reproduce in this historical number many other old things which research of the issues of our own magazine have brought to light, or, rather, brought back to vivid memory. Almost 20 years of trade paper publishing naturally gives opportunity for printing things about relatively older events in many issues and we have ourselves been surprised many times to discover, or, we might say, re-discover facts little known to the great majority comprising the industry today. The electrotype herewith is an example of much which causes us to transgress from the subject.

Fortuna

Stolzenberg being the first of the names by which this machine is customarily referred to by members of the trade, it is likely that those searching for this treatment would turn to the later alphabetical classification, but as the former was once the name of an entirely different machine we place here our historical identification of the Stolzenberg-Fortuna typewriter which made its bow to the world's business public the fore part of 1923.

It is a standard type of machine of front stroke, single shift and 84 characters with all requirements of modern typewriter construction, including an interchangeable carriage. The machine

is manufactured in the munitions factory of J. P. Sauer & Son, of Suhl, Germany, who have accorded sole selling rights for their Fortuna typewriter to the well-known Fabrik Stolzenberg, Oos, Baden, Germany, who have presented it to the industry as the Stolzenberg-Fortuna.

The Stolzenberg Company, prominent manufacturers of office furniture, filing equipment and specialties, were, before taking this machine, among the most important distributors of typewriters in Germany. They were the original agents for the Corona, selling that machine in its earlier days as the Piccola, and also very successful as distributors for the Oliver, which fact is recorded under the heading of Stolzenberg, by which name the Oliver was known in Germany. There is a similarity of finish between the older Stolzenberg and the present Stolzenberg-Fortuna in the olive green enamelled color in which the latter appears.

Fontana

A standard, front stroke writing machine of single shift and 42 keys, with removable carriage and the various other modern features that contribute to the typewriter of today describes the Fontana. It appeared in 1921 and as the post-war effort of the well-known electrical and automobile supply manufacturers, S. A. Fratelli Fontana, Turin, Italy, has since been transformed into the Hesperia elsewhere classified.

Fountain

We are not quite sure by just what other name this machine was known, or, rather, what other typewriter was sold by a particular distributor as the Fountain. It had a type-wheel, universal keyboard, wrote through a ribbon and was a double shift machine. Its price was $35 and is said to have been put out for Siegel, Cooper & Co., the once "Big Store" on Sixth Avenue in New York where "Meet me at the Fountain" had something to do with the name of the typewriter they handled.

Frister & Rossmann

Acknowledged as the first typewriter manufactured in Germany, the machine bearing the name of the manufactures was presented to the buying public in that country in 1888. It was made by Messrs. Frister & Rossmann of Berlin and the product was the same as the American machine called the Caligraph which has already been described in this narrative. It enjoyed a very healthy German sale and established the makers securely as prominent members of the writing machine industry. However, they later abandoned this product and attached their name to a portable typewriter mentioned elsewhere, the Senta, which they continue to manufacture in large quantity.

The firm of Messrs. Frister & Rossmann dates back to 1864, but before that they had run a small repair shop for sewing machines; this was located in the neighborhood of the present premises. They inaugurated the association for manufacturing of a sewing machine with rotation hook and were the first to build a sewing machine in Germany. Development was rapid and in 1871 the firm was changed to an A. G. (Limited Company), building all sorts of sewing machines up to the most modern types which met with favor and consequent good demand all over the world.

As noted above, Messrs. Frister & Rossmann were also the pioneers in German typewriter manufacture, their Frister & Rossmann Schnellschreibmaschinen (Tachygraph) meeting with a success equal to their other products. Authorities in government such as the German General Post Office, the Kulturministerium, the Justizministerium, bought from the beginning, and industrial firms and others were constant purchasers. The Deutsche Reichspost had hundreds of the machines in use.

Franklin

An all metal machine, except the key tops, platen and feed rolls, the Franklin was of ribbon writing, typebar, shift key construction. The keyboard was in semi-circular form in universal

arrangement and the bars struck directly downward from a horizontal position when at rest. The No. 7 was the big seller at home, while the No. 8 with four additional characters sold overseas. It weighed 13 pounds, the two models mentioned retailing, respectively, at $75 and $80. The manufacture of the Franklin was the nucleus of the enterprise which is still well known to the entire industry, the Victor Typewriter Company.

The Franklin was another of the inventions of the well-known and exceedingly versatile Wellington P. Kidder, inventor of the Empire and Wellington, famous for his activity with the Noiseless and more recently with the Rochester Portable. The keyboard of the first Franklins had only 26 keys, employing a double shift, but was later enlarged and improved to a 42-key, single-shift, 84-character machine. The last model was the No. 10, brought

THE NEW FRANKLIN

out in 1904 as the work of Mr. Kidder in affiliation with Walter J. Barron, formerly of the Remington and Caligraph, and manufactured by the Franklin Typewriter Company, New York, established in 1892. This was called the New Franklin.

Fox

William R. Fox organized the Fox Machine Company of Grand Rapids, Michigan, in 1892, incorporating with capital stock of $150,000. Experimental work on a typewriter invented by Glenn

THE "BLIND" FOX

J. Barrett was taken up in 1898 and in 1902 the Fox Typewriter Company was organized as a separate institution for manufacture of the Fox typewriter. Mr. Fox was president and A. J. Williams figured prominently in the early days of this endeavor.

The initial Fox typewriters were so-called blind writers, departing from the carriage shift or basket shift in arrival at capital letter printing through shifting of the platen only. Another innovation of the day was provision for writing either horizontally or perpendicularly the full width or length of the paper. The No. 4 was the one of this type mostly heard of, it being ribbon writing, had the universal keyboard in four banks, automatic line spacer, etc., and was listed at $100.

In February, 1906, the first of the Fox visible writers came out, improved models appearing from time to time until February, 1912, when the No. 24 was offered; this was the largest seller of the various models. The machine of 1908 was sold in some territories as the Rapid.

The Fox Visible introduced one very pronounced peculiarity—its typebars were not all of one length, half of them lying behind the other half in the basket and the bars of the front portion being bent in correspondingly numerous ways to avoid confliction with the others. However, we hasten to say, this innovation in no way mitigated against successful and rapid operation of the Fox Visible.

THE FOX VISIBLE

The coming out of the Fox Portable, the later name for the Baby Fox illustrated herewith, met with legal action by the Corona Typewriter Company on account of a folding feature and its manufacture was discontinued, to be followed by the Fox Sterling non-folding single shift machine mentioned elsewhere.

When war broke in 1914, the Fox typewriter plant was partially closed and ever since then it has been an uncertain element in the industry. Mr. Fox retired from the typewriter enterprise in January, 1915, going back to the Fox Machine Company, the manufacture of whose products, including multiple drills, was removed to Jackson, Mich.

A new Fox typewriter company was organized late in 1915 with capital of $150,000 to acquire the patents and manufacturing facilities of the old company. This was headed by Earl Stokoe, Irving Frank and others, including F. I. Chichester, a banker. In November, 1917, the Baby Fox, the portable machine, was introduced; this was the invention of Henry P. Nordmark. The next month Irving Frank sold his interest and retired. Receivership overtook the undertaking and W. A. Papworth was appointed by the court to take charge on May 19, 1921. Foreclosure by note holders came after this and the Fox typewriter enterprise was lost to the industry.

THE BABY FOX

German Imperial

Not of long duration as to existence in the field of writing machines was the German Imperial, invented and manufactured by Heinrich Kochendörfer of Leipzig, who also was responsible for the Eureka typewriter. This Imperial of German origin should not be confused with the better known machine of the same name of English manufacture and described in a later classification. The German Imperial was not unlike the Blickensderfer in that it employed a similar type wheel and ink roll mechanism.

Gerda

Brought out in 1921, the Gerda writing machine, the product of George Emig of Berlin, was intended to serve the blind and one armed veterans of the late war. Numbers of machines were delivered. The Gerda functions by means of a type wheel but instead of the usual keyboard has an indicator scale upon which the entire hand rests and following a movement right or left till the desired character is reached is depressed by the same hand and impression made.

Garbell

This was a machine of the portable variety for which manufacture was started in Chicago, Ill., by the Garbell Typewriter Company, at 1812-14 Ellen Street in March, 1919. It weighed 5½ pounds in its case, stood only four inches high and had three banks of keys with double shift. The Garbell was of typebar mechanism similar to the earlier Empire but actuated by gear movement, the first of its kind to eliminate springs. The inventor was Max Garbell, who is still in the typewriter industry in Chicago. Financial difficulties forced the Garbell enterprise into liquidation in July, 1923, Henry K. Gilbert, formerly president of the Oliver Typewriter Company, being appointed receiver.

Gardner

An odd machine writing from a type-wheel, having only 13 keys but writing 78 characters. The first Gardner appeared in England in 1890, the same device being made and sold in France as the Victorieuse and in Germany as the Victoria. This typewriter was the invention of John Gardner of Manchester, England.

Gisela

Günther & Co., Berlin, made a typewriter called the Gisela which, however, is not today being manufactured. It originated in 1921 and was a moderately priced three bank, double shift machine of small size and orthodox lines in its class.

Glashütte

A single shift, four row keyboard machine of excellent design and construction and promising a healthy sale is the Glashütte typewriter. The machine has all the usual high grade requirements of the modern standard writing instrument and is composed of almost 900 fewer parts than the average machine of its class.

The Glashütte is a throughly high grade mechanism and is manufactured by people who are familiar with such production. Glashütte is the home of Germany's clock and watch manufacturing industry and one of that country's most important industrial centres. With the post-war lull in the watch business, the local government brought most of the important watch manufacturers together and assigned to each a portion of the manufacture of a typewriter named after the municipality. It constitutes a genuine co-operative effort, the first of the kind in the annals of the typewriter industry.

Gourland

It is due M. J. Gourland to say as a first reference to this machine that he has been untiring in his endeavor to get the Gourland typewriter onto the market. In substantiation of the merit

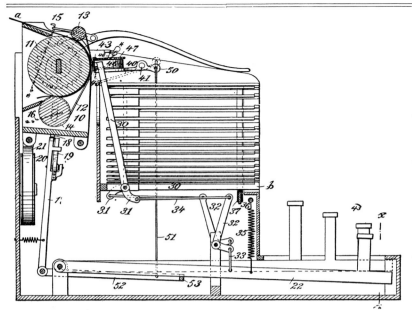

Grundy

Nothing in the way of illustration is available in the way of pictorial presentation of the Grundy typewriter except the accompanying reproduction of a drawing taken from the records of the United States Patent Office at Washington, D. C. Through the kindness of the Royal Typewriter Company, who used it in the book which they recently published and which we mentioned in an introductory paragraph, the drawing is reprinted here. It represents the patent issued on January 18, 1887, to Arthur Grundy, of Whitestone, New York, for a front stroke typewriter of standard pattern. A firm of Prouty & Hynes also took patents for a similar machine, differing in the typebar intermediate actuating mechanism. The Prouty & Hynes had a push link connection between the key lever and the typebar, whereas the Grundy here illustrated had an intermediate bell crank lever and two links to effect the same purpose. Neither of these machines was manufactured.

PHOTOGRAPH FROM THE U. S. PATENT OFFICE GAZETTE

---

of the product it must also be said that Charles Spiro is responsible for the refinements in design of this forerunner of portable typewriters with four banks of keys and single shift. A novel device appears in this machine in the sublever pivots *below* the key levers, thus reducing the height of the machine materially without affecting its efficient operation. It also contains the novel

device of automatic marginal stops, set by the act of placing the paper guide fingers at the front of the platen to hold the edges of the paper. The Gourland was first announced in April, 1920, by the Gourland Typewriter Corp., then at 120 Broadway, New York City. The factory was and is located in Brooklyn and several thousand machines have been made and sold, a good portion through the instrumentality of W. W. Ramer, former American sales representative.

Granville Automatic

A 42 key, 84 character machine, similar to the Rapid but improved considerably. Its birth was in 1896, the invention of Bern. Granville of Dayton, Ohio, also one of the inventors of the

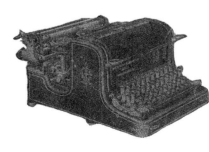

Rapid. Attempts were originally made by the Granville Manufacturing Company and the Mossberg & Granville Manufacturing Company of Providence, R. I., to bring out the machine, but without success. The inventor later took his machine to London, where the Granville Automatic Typewriter Syndicate, Ltd., was formed and following a series of untoward manipulations in the British company's shares, the Granville Automatic disappeared forever from the typewriter stage.

Graphic

An indicator type of machine was the Graphic typewriter. It was made along the lines of the Hall, utilizing only one hand for operation while the other found the point of designation for the various characters. It was manufactured in Berlin, Germany, by C. F. Kindermann & Company, making its appearance in 1895.

Haberl

There was a typewriter of this name on exhibition as part of a 1907 typewriter display at the Venice, Italy, gathering of writing machines mentioned elsewhere in this anniversary number, but no details are available.

Halda

The first Swedish writing machine ever produced, appearing in 1896 and being a machine something along the lines of the Densmore. It was manufactured by the Halda A. B. of Sweden and invented by H. Hammarlund. Halda Model 4, a considerably improved machine over the first, was brought out in 1902, later the visible writing product being manufactured and sold to users.

Hall

This machine, made in two models, and invented by Thomas Hall of Brooklyn, New York, came onto the market in 1880, though records of its invention in primary principle bear date

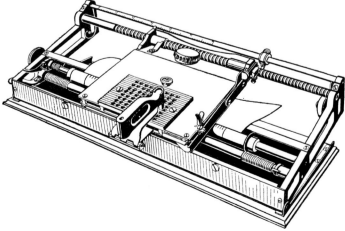

LINE DRAWING OF THE HALL TYPEWRITER SUPPLIED BY C. V. ODEN

several years previous. Other mention is made of this machine in a paragraph devoted to the earlier efforts preliminary to the actual birth of the typewriter industry 50 years ago, when the first commercially practical writing machine was offered for public sale. The Hall was a small machine of unusual construction, differing from all others which preceded it in its writing from a rectangular rubber plate with nine characters in a row, there being nine rows in all. Thomas Hall died in Brooklyn on November 19, 1911, at the age of 77 years.

Hammond

Any narration of the story of the development of the typewriter would be incomplete if it did not contain the interesting phase covered by the development of the Hammond typewriter.

THE No. 12 MODEL

One of the first persons to appreciate the magnitude of the possibilities in the typewriter was James B. Hammond, who had been educated in the universities of America and Europe in preparation for the ministry. He had served in the Civil War as a correspondent for the *New York Tribune* and had served for a time as a court reporter.

In 1880, soon after the Remington typewriter had become commercially practical, Mr. Hammond began experimenting in an effort to produce a typewriter which would turn out what he aspired to make better looking work than it was possible to produce on the early Remington. He it was who conceived the idea of a typewriter with an automatic printing mechanism which would result in every character being printed with the same force or blow. With this as his prime motive and the conspicuous work of E. J. Manning there was developed the fundamental principles which have formed the basis of the Hammond typewriter as it is known today with the exclusive features of interchangeable type and variable spacing between the characters plus the automatic type impression which makes it possible for the novice to write all of his characters with uniform appearance. The first Hammonds were manufactured for the inventor in the factory of the old and still existing Garvin Machine Company of New York City, E. J. Manning starting his typewriter experience with that concern in 1886 as a mechanic.

Mr. Hammond studied with great intensity the subject of typewriter keyboards. He arrived at the conclusion that the arrangement of the keys used on the early Remington was far from being the best that could be devised. He, accordingly, developed a keyboard which he called the "Ideal," in which the characters most used were put in such positions that the fingers of the operator could manipulate the keys with much greater speed than in the arrangement of the American standard keyboard, and Mr. Hammond considered that he was justified in his position because of the fact that at that time different countries were calling for different arrangements of the keys—which resulted in the variations now to be found in the French keyboard, for example, as compared with the American keyboard.

However, Mr. Hammond entered the field too late to impress his ideas upon the other manufacturers, because the public had already been educated to the keyboard which has now become known as the standard keyboard. The Hammond Ideal was, however, largely adopted by early users of the typewriter and many users in all countries of the world still insist upon using that style of keyboard. The Hammond Company, however, no longer makes the Ideal keyboard except upon special request, having some years ago practically standardized upon the universal arrangement of characters.

MULTIPLEX IDEAL

The unique beauty of the work produced by the Hammond combined with its other distinctive features won instant popularity for the machine and Mr. Hammond who had always been a poor boy witnessed an original investment of $5,000 grow in value until he became a millionaire. He was much in the public eye and up to the time of his death, on January 27, 1913, was well known both in Europe and America particularly for his philanthropies and somewhat for his eccentricities.

Following the tendency of the times for lightness and compactness in typewriting machines, the Hammond Company has accomplished within the last year the novel result of condensing the features of its standard machine into a folding typewriter which weighs 8½ pounds, but which, nevertheless, has the full capacity of the large machine—taking any width of paper and carrying two sets of type, with variable spacing between the characters. In these features the

NEW FOLDING PORTABLE

Hammond occupies a special field which is without competition. The machine is sought particularly by private users and by professional men such as engineers, chemists, physicians, teachers, writers, etc., etc., besides enjoying great popularity in commercial offices where a special machine is desired for tabulations or charts and particularly for executive correspondence where distinctiveness is desired. Advent of an aluminum model weighing 11½ pounds in 1915 and the round front Multiplex Hammond later in the same year are familiar to all followers of typewriter events.

The story of the Hammond is one of the romances of American business and is another illustration of how the ideas of one man carefully nurtured may make a tremendous impression not only upon the generation in which he lived, but all succeeding generations. Plans for broad extension of the Hammond enterprise were involved in the formation, in October, 1921, of the Hammond Typewriter Corporation, a $2,500,000 company of which Neal D. Becker is the president. Taking over of the old Hammond company and the front-stroke typewriter formerly known as the Federal were included.

NEW REGULAR MULTIPLEX

Hammonia

Patented in 1884 by H. A. H. Guhl, according to the records of the Scientific Museum of South Kensington, London, England, the Hammonia typewriter had a dial for location of the characters and embossed the latter in suitable paper for use by the blind. It was never developed along commercial lines.

Harris Visible

This machine was made by the Harris Typewriter Company of Fond du Lac, Wisconsin, exclusively for marketing by the famous mail order house of Sears, Roebuck & Company of Chicago. Not a dissimilar machine was produced under another name and sold through other channels. In fact, the Harris later became the Rex, the details appearing under the heading of Demountable.

Hassia

Jean Volker & Co., Neu-Isenburg, Germany, made a standard typewriter from 1904 to 1908 which was called the Hassia. It retailed in German money of that time at 350 Marks, was a front stroke, typebar, removable platen and carriage machine and had a novel feature in the hinged carriage which swung back for easy and accessible cleaning. This machine was later secured by the Weilwerke A-G., and resembles the machine today marketed as the Torpedo.

Helios

Appearing first in 1909, the Helios typewriter is one of the most novel and ingenious of the kind constructed to sell at the more moderate price, the selling price of the regular product approxi-

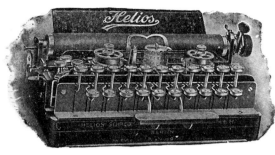

mating $20. It secures impression from a type wheel writing through a ribbon but its keyboard is arranged in only two straight rows and with a capacity of 90 characters, utilizing what is believed to be the first of its kind, a triple shift.

The Helios, of course, has been greatly improved since its initial appearance and it has also had a varied experience. Originally produced by Justin Wm. Bamberger & Co. of Munich, Germany, it was later transferred to the Kanzler Schreibmaschinen A. G. of Berlin, and upon the failure of the latter company it was taken over by the firm of A. Ney & Co. of Berlin, who are marketing the machine today as the Helios-Klimax. The same machine has also been known as the Ultima.

The Helios was once manufactured by Helios Schreibmaschinen Ges. m. b. H., Berlin, S. W. 68, Friedrichstr. 200, according to an early announcement in this publication, being sold then in England at £7.10.0.

Hartford

Our recollections and observations induce us to point out as an example of typewriters which were put onto the market at retail prices too low to insure success, the Hartford typewriter. It was a typebar, ribbon writing, double keyboard machine with features commending it to a place in the $100 class but upon which a price of only $50 was placed. The writer of these lines is strongly inclined to believe that it disappeared in large measure because the margin or profit was insufficient, just as did many others

THE HARTFORD TYPEWRITER

for the same reason.

The Hartford was a blind writer, having mechanism very similar to the Caligraph. It introduced several new instances of change in keyboard arrangement which outlived the machine and which are in universal use today. John M. Fairfield, of Hartford, Conn., was the inventor, his earlier experience with the Caligraph leading him to creation of a machine of his own which he anticipated giving to the public at one-half of the then accepted price for a standard machine. The factory, first at Hartford, was later moved to Cleveland, Ohio, and a new and improved model was brought out which was called the Cleveland. There was also a Model 3 Hartford, which was a four bank machine with single shift and writing 88 characters. The original product was introduced in 1894.

Hermes

A machine of likely appearance, substantial construction and several features distinctively its own, perfected for the market in late 1921 as one of Switzerland's real efforts in writing machine invention is the Hermes. It is a single shift, 46-key machine and has all the usual accoutrements of modern demand. A particularly novel and efficient column finder and tabulator is a part of the equipment of this Swiss typewriter, the product of E. Paillard & Co., St. Croix, Switzerland, a firm more than 100 years old and famed for its precision instruments.

Hesperia

This machine is standard in every particular, selling in its native country at a retail price of Lire 1,900. The manufacturers are Compagnia Italiana Macchine da Scrivere "Hesperia," Strada

Borgaro 27, Turin, Italy, a change appearing in August, 1923, from F. I. L. I. S. Fabrica Italiana Lavorazioni in Serie.

One of Italy's more recent ventures in the typewriter industry is the Hesperia, a high grade machine in every respect, with single shift and 84 characters. Not only has the Hesperia most of the requirements of modern writing machines, but it has several features distinctively its own.

The sales campaign for the Hesperia is headed by J. Colloridi, a European typewriter man of high repute who is well experienced in the marketing of machines, American and otherwise, in France and Italy.

Horton

Again resort is taken to reproduction of a drawing in conveyance of illustration of the patent taken in 1885 by the inventor of the Horton typewriter. This reprint is also shown as a result of consent by the Royal Typewriter Company, they having taken it from the records of the United States Patent Office and loaned the cut for use in this historical compilation. The machine was made by the Horton Typewriter Company of Toronto, Canada, the first typewriter produced in the Dominion. It was a typebar machine of full keyboard and though possessing considerable merit did not long survive. E. E. Horton took out the patent pictured by the accompanying drawing on September 18, 1883.

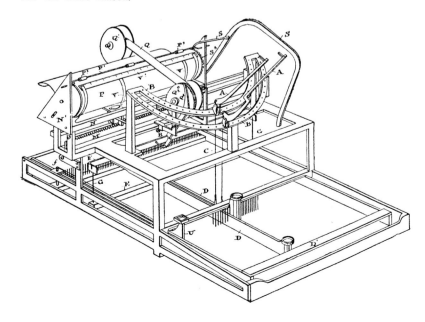

THE FRAME CONSTRUCTION OF THE HORTON TYPEWRITER

(From photograph reproduced from Patent Office Gazette Publication)

Heroine

Model A of the Heroine typewriter, the most recent product of Franz Heumann, Haueneberstein b. Baden-Baden, Germany, is a standard front stroke writer with the usual modern features and refinements and listed at a moderate price. The machine is manufactured in Mr. Heumann's modern factory at Haueneberstein, makes an attractive appearance, is well constructed, nicely finished and enjoys a healthy internal German sale and activity in export markets.

This is an enterprise which has developed from a very small beginning. Mr. Heumann, the son of a Rhineland farmer, devoted himself with full interest to the construction of machines after short technical study. He was only 19 years old when he was already the manager of an important machine factory. Shortly after that he went abroad to gather more knowledge of foreign business organizations and with an open interest for everything new and everything that had a future. He went into the office equipment industry, and held leading and responsible posts in several of the first-class enterprises of this industry. A few years later he laid the foundation for his important enterprise whereby he has particularly devoted himself to the construction of typewritetrs and their export.

Hooven

The Hooven automatic typewriter really appeared first on the market in 1912 in the shape of its forerunner, the National automatic. It was manufactured by a company bearing the Hooven

name in Cincinnati, Ohio. At the head of the enterprise, a man who pioneered in the field of automatic machines and later joined the Hooven Company, was M. E. Roberts, now manager in Chicago for the Remington Company. This Mr. Roberts should not be confused with, nor was he related to, the late L. R. Roberts, inventor of the Underwood automatic typewriter and likewise a pioneer in this field. Outright sale of Hooven machines through branches and other distributing agencies never seemed to work quite right, and today the Hooven Automatic Typewriter Co., of Hamilton, Ohio, the present manufacturers of the machine, are supplying the product chiefly for job work in automatically typewritten letters.

The Hooven, although adaptable to many different makes, is usually used in combination with Underwood typewriters. It is operated electrically and utilizes a master perforated roll on the order of the player piano system.

Ideal

Seidel & Naumann, of Dresden, Saxony, Germany, an institution founded by Bruno Naumann and who died in 1903, are manufacturers of the Ideal typewriter. Machines for many languages

have been made from the first, a record of 30,000 typewriters marketed having been reached by the end of 1906. In that year a machine called the Ideal Polyglot, having two keyboards giving a total of 126 characters and selling at 550 marks, was put out. The No. 4 Ideal was placed on the market in October, 1909.

THE ORIGINAL IDEAL TYPEWRITER, DESIGNED BY E. E. BARNEY

Seidel & Naumann A-G., also prominent manufacturers of bicycles and sewing machines, brought out their first typewriter product in 1900. It had a single shift, writing 84 characters from typebars which operated by front stroke in absolute visibility.

A fact not generally known, never recorded to our knowledge in any trade paper or historical treatment, was the connection of E. E. Barney with Seidel & Naumann from 1899 to 1901. Mr. Barney, who is now in New York in charge of experimental and development work for the Remington Typewriter Co., not only designed the Ideal typewriter but he also tooled that well-known machine and personally directed the start of its production.

The famous Seidel & Naumann firm very early displayed great initiative in the distribution of their product and enjoyed a consequent exceedingly prosperous export trade. They were among the earliest German manufacturers of typewriters to devote attention to marketing outside the boundaries of their own country. The Seidel & Naumann people became great specialists in the adaptation of their machine to every language and special keyboard arrangements and actions, this effort eventuating in the making of their Ideal-Polyglot machine for writing of two or more languages on the same typewriter. Combinations of German and Russian and many others were supplied. Three languages can be written on one machine when all caps are used, like Hebrew, Russian and German, reverse escapement and carriage action being a mechanical feature for Hebraic and similar writing worthy of note.

In 1913 an entirely new Ideal typewriter was prepared for the market, this being a standard front stroke machine of present-day accepted principle. Three different models of the newer machine have been manufactured, the last one appearing during the current year with many improvements and refinements. The Ideal is a thoroughly high class writing instrument and has been accepted universally as such, to the extent that it has been undertaken for production by a prominent group of manufacturers in France.

Imperial

The inception of the Imperial typewriter in England was due to the inventive genius of Hidalgo Moya, a typewriter expert, combined with the financial support of a well-known business man,

J. G. Chattaway, who in 1902 commenced work on a typewriter in a small factory in Leicester, where the first models were made. The present Imperial Typewriter Company, Ltd., is the successor to the earlier enterprise known as the Moya Typewriter Co.

The venture underwent some years of hard struggle and vicissitude owing to the lack of experienced technical typewriter men and of trained typewriter labor in England, but always it grew, steadily, if slowly, and in 1908 took over larger premises. During that year the Imperial typewriter was invented by Mr. Moya and a limited company was registered, more adequately to exploit the typewriter trade and put this new machine on the market. The new typewriter was unique, being somewhat unconventional in design—but unconventionality backed by real scientific and technical reasons is the mark of progress.

In 1911 a marked step forward was taken when the services of Eric J. Pilblad were secured as general manager. Mr. Pilblad has had an exceptional training, not only as a practical engineer, but as a successful organizer in the mass production of component parts of typewriters, adding machines, etc. He was discovered making rifle sights for the Canadian Government and his experience has been of the greatest value to the Imperial company in perfecting the production of typewriters in Leicester. In the same year a new factory in North Evington was built by J. Wallis Goddard, to which the manufacture was transferred.

In 1920 more accommodation became necessary and the present specially designed factory in North Evington was erected on very modern lines, enabling work to be carried on under the most suitable conditions possible, combined with every convenience for the welfare of the employees. Leicester now manufactures a typewriter with 96 characters which gives all the signs and requirements so necessary in British business. It is, in fact, a real British typewriter, entirely built by Leicester workers to suit English requirements. It is interesting to note that as a corollary to the manufacture there of typewriters, Leicester has the most completely equipped steel type-making plant in the Empire, machinery being used at the North Evington Works that is certainly not surpassed, if equalled, any where in the world.

Model "B" Imperial was introduced in April, 1915. In 1919, the Model "D" was initially presented to the trade, ten years after the first of the machines of the same general nature came out. How-

IMPERIAL WITH STRAIGHT LINE KEYBOARD

ever, there was a considerable departure in the last named for the reason that it had a straight line keyboard instead of the circular construction which had long marked the Imperial typewriter. At the same time that Model "B" was introduced in 1915 a lightweight machine also appeared; this was called Model "C." The Imperial was at one time sold in France as the "Typo." The German distributors of the British made Imperial typewriter sold the product within their territory as the Ajax.

The Imperial Typewriter Co., Ltd., whose sales offices are located at 260, High Holborn, London, W. C. 1, are just getting out a portable Imperial. A newly developed alloy is used in reduction of weight, but otherwise the lightweight machine is in general appearance much like the standard Imperial. The new portable is visible writing, has 84 characters together with many other modern requirements and will sell in a carrying case for £16.16.0.

International

This was the name of a typewriter which bears the date of 1889 as its beginning and it was invented by Lucien Stephen Crandall, who was responsible for other creations including that which was

named after him. This was a blind writer of the typebar variety, a notable addition to other famous contributions to typewriter history by the same inventor. Although the International had numerous distinctive and meritorious points in its favor it did not seem to gain much public favor and eventually disappeared from the writing machine arena. It was a shift key machine of 38 keys writing 76 characters, was priced at $100 and was manufactured at Parish, N. Y.

Invicta

In November, 1921, this machine was first presented for consideration of the members of the writing machine industry. It is the invention of Ing. G. Giachero, Torino, Italy, and while not extensively pushed up to the present time meets requirements of the day in standard typewriters. It has 44 keys, four banks with one shift, interchangeable carriage, built-in tabulator and weighs 10 kilos.

The concern which owns the Invicta was lately transformed into the Socienta Anonima Invicta-Torino for the purpose of executing plans for making the machine as developed in the factory of Ing. Guiseppe Giachero. The latest model, which has been worked out during the last six months, is the result of long experience in other typewriter factories and incorporates every required feature. It has a three-piece demountable typebar system, ball-bearing, silent moving carriage and a successful retarder in the typebar's stroke. The factory equipment includes the most improved special machine tools and the Invicta will be priced to meet competition.

Jackson

This typewriter was first making itself known in 1898. It was a typebar, pad writing, double shift machine of standard quality, priced at $100. It had 42 keys in universal arrangement and the

typebars were arranged in semi-circular manner similar to others of the time. The writing was accomplished, not through pressure of the keys which merely brought the type to the printing position, but through action of a separate bar which furnished the required pressure. This rather destroyed the manifolding usefulness of the Jackson. It was invented by Jos. H. Jackson of Hamilton, Ontario, and manufactured by the Jackson Typewriter Company of Boston, Mass.

Japanese

There was publication in the June, 1919, issue of this magazine of the preparation for the market by the Japanese Typewriter Company of Tokyo, Japan, of a typewriter. It was described as having 3,000 characters and priced in Japanese money the equivalent of $240. The same company are credited with creation of a typewriter for the Chinese language, or, perhaps more properly speaking, an adaptation of characters representing Chinese, as is also true of the Japanese typewriter. The Chinese product is said to write 4,000 characters. The Japanese typewriter is on the market today and enjoying a wide sale where such a native language writing machine is required. Although speed is naturally sacrificed, ability to write so many different characters carries an important appeal.

Japy

Japy Frères & Cie have been devoting time and energy to the manufacture of a typewriter in France since September, 1910, when a machine of original invention and manufacture in America was taken overseas and the enterprise formed for production of the first writing machine to be made in and marketed from that country.

The Japy company is a large institution in Beaucourt, France, manufacturing a large variety of different kinds of machinery, of which the typewriter department is one. The factory was under enemy occupation during the war, but at this date is proceeding as before and producing satisfactory quantities and enjoying a good sale within France and in several outside countries. Several speed contests for French typists have been won on the Japy, a machine of standard construction with four banks of keys and single shift, front stroke, etc.

The present-day Japy typewriter is a thoroughly high grade machine, durable, attractive in appearance, simple in construction, convenient in facilities of operation and rapid in operation. It is equipped with a decimal tabulator and is made in various carriage widths and different type styles. The Japy is today used in many government offices in France and by large numbers of important commercial institutions. Branches are maintained throughout that country. Although typewriters are but a part of the great Japy Frères activity, the huge factory at Beaucourt is delivering a greatly improved standard writing machine.

Jewett

A full keyboard machine, with a key for every character, the Jewett, was introduced in 1892. It was what in those days was called by the sellers of visibles a blind writer. It had a carriage which required raising for inspection of the work, in other words. Also, to go through more of the category, the writing was invisible at the time of writing. It resembled the Smith Premier of the time to a great extent and, like the latter, met demands of the day by changing to a visible **writer** and was renamed the Jewett Visible. In 1904 the machine was equipped with the Gorin tabulator. The

THE JEWETT TYPEWRITER

Jewett was the invention of George A. Jewett, who was also president of the Jewett Typewriter Company of Des Moines, Iowa, producers of the machine. In April, 1909, the same gentleman went to England, where it was reported at the time that he had arranged for manufacture of his invention at Birmingham. It was assembled and sold in Germany, where it was known as the Jewett-Germania, by J. Scheffler-Hoppenhöfer, Sundern, Westphalia, the last product, like the American Visible Jewett, being a "sight writer" of front stroke, interchangeable ribbon spool, single shift machine.

Junior

This is not to be confused with a machine called the Remington Jr. referred to elsewhere, the typewriter named Junior without out prefix being the invention of Chas. A. Bennett, of Dover, N. J. It was priced at $15 and was offered in

September, 1907, by the Junior Typewriter Company with headquarters at 97 Worth Street, New York City. It claimed a writing capacity of 80 words a minute, was equipped for four languages, had 84 characters, measured 10 inches long, 5 inches wide and 2 inches high in its leatherette case. The Junior, which wrote from a pad, appeared after acquisition by new interests under the name of the inventor.

Jundt

Alfred C. Jundt, 523 Richard Street, Dayton, Ohio., was reported in the April, 1908, issue of this trade paper as the moving spirit in a project to organize a company in that city to manufacture a typewriter which had been invented by a Wisconsin jeweller of unrevealed identity at the time, but which was to be named after the financial backer. It did not materialize, as such, but the jeweller mentioned was Mr. Molle, now deceased. Although the later product was not quite the same machine, the Molle typewriter was a similar invention which was manufactured at Oshkosh, Wis. It is later referred to in this narrative.

Kanzler

The Aktiengesellschaft für Schreibmaschinen Industrie, Berlin, Germany, began manufacturing typewriters in 1903. The Kanzler was the product, a machine differing in principle from others but for which a broad market was developed up until a comparatively

short time ago, when it is understood effort was terminated. The last model, in which a number of improvements were incorporated, was offered as the New Model IV in April, 1910. It was a four-bank, single shift visible writing machine, with a typebar action along the lines of the older Empire, Adler and Wellington, and enjoyed the distinction of being the first German writing machine to be manufactured by a company exclusively operating in typewriter production. Previous German machines were produced by makers chiefly of bicycles, sewing machines, etc. The Kanzler was once called the Hanson and it was for a time sold in England as the Chancellor.

Kappel

This is a typewriter product of comparatively recent introduction, the first model being brought out in the spring of 1914 by the Maschinenfabrik Kappel A-G., of Chemnitz-Kappel, Germany. The enterprise dates from its founding in 1860 and is now known all over the world for precision machinery, having a

THE LATEST KAPPEL, MODEL NO. 66

reputation in that line which accounts for knowledge valuable in the production of a typewriter. The Kappel has enjoyed in its development the backing of manufacturing knowledge applicable to such a product and no expense has been spared in making a quiet, smooth running, solid frame, fine appearing, simply constructed and up-to-date machine.

The keyboard of the Kappel consists of 44 keys, one shift key giving a total of 88 characters, the carriage runs on ball bearings and is well balanced. One of the latest and most outstanding improvements is in the quiet return of the carriage, secured by an ingeniously constructed mechanism which, when the carriage is pulled back for a new line, prevents the customary gripping into the escapement by which noise is created. The special ribbon drive works only when typebars are in action and the Kappel with a normal 25 cm. platen takes paper of the same size which normally requires a platen 30 cm. wide.

The above and other modern arrangements are handily simple for operation by the typist, the machine is so constructed as to make replacements easy and quick and the Kappel factory claim that nothing but the best materials are used in manufacture. Carriage lengths of 25, 30, 40 and 50 cm. are supplied and single and decimal tabulators are available.

Keystone

A truss-wheel carried the type on this machine, a ribbon writing, low priced, double shift key, three bank, visible typewriter. It appeared in 1899, was manufactured by the Keystone Typewriter Company of New York in a factory at Harrisburg, Pa., and was designed to cater to a lowered price field. The type were interchangeable and it retailed at $35.

Kneist

An indicator type of machine resembling the Hall introduced in 1893. The Kneist typewriter wrote 81 characters with a keyboard arranged also in like manner to the aforementioned machine. It was one of the earliest German machines, the invention of Otto F. Mayer and J. Funcke of Berlin. It was named, however, after the manufacturer, Otto Kneist, of Hanover, Germany.

Knickerbocker

We are unable to locate much information regarding this machine, as to what it was like or where it came from earlier, but in November, 1912, P. C. Knox, Jr., H. W. Morgan and Austin Herr acquired the assets of the Knickerbocker Typewriter Company with a factory at Niantic, Conn. The announcement was made then that the name would be changed and that after a reorganization of the acquisition it would be known as the Defiance Typewriter Company, but nothing further was heard of the undertaking that is identifiable.

Kosmopolit

An indicator type of machine dating from 1888 which permitted actual writing with only one hand that purported to be more for quality work rather than speed was called the Kosmopolit. A model was also made for use by the blind and there is record of the price in an announcement in 1907 that carried what is equivalent today to $38. This machine was manufactured by Guhl & Harbeck, of Hamburg, Germany, also makers of sewing machines.

Lambert

A slow writing machine of low price but novel construction, the type of which were all arranged on a common carrier of hard rubber which was pressed down for the desired letter and imprint made. The Lambert bore the name of the inventor, Frank Lambert of Brooklyn, N. Y. It enjoyed rather an active sale. The same machine was manufactured in Germany by the German Gramophone Company and so far as our knowledge goes is still being produced in France by Sydney Herbert of Dieppe.

Lasar

A visible writing, shift key typewriter was manufactured somewhere around 1898 to 1900 by the Lasar Typewriter Company of St. Louis, Mo. No very serious marketing campaign, however, was ever undertaken, though not an inconsiderable number of machines were made. We are not quite clear on what took place, but we recall some connection of J. E. Albright, proprietor of the St. Louis Typewriter Exchange, with Lasar typewriters; possibly in disposition of a surplus. P. K. Lawrence, at present living at the Illinois Athletic Club in Chicago and whose initials were adopted for the "P. K." chewing gum when Wrigley's recently put that brand on the market, is understood to have had something to do with the making and selling of Lasar typewriters. We might also refer particularly inquisitive readers to Harry Ballard and Herb Newport for what they may know about this machine; at least we are inclined to believe that the Lasar filled an important place in the industry as a "skate," but we prefer not to be asked what is meant by the term.

Leggatt

A portable typewriter of this name was the object of no inconsiderable interest on the part of men of the trade who inspected it in 1922. In June of the same year the Leggatt Portable Typewriter Corporation was formed with authorized capital of 100,000 shares of common stock of no par value. It is understood that the assets were acquired by interests affiliated with Rochester Industries, a corporation of which reference has appeared in these columns in connection with description of the Rochester Portable typewriter, which is similar to the machine known as Leggatt.

Lilliput

This is the name of a German machine actually made and sold for some time by Justin Wm. Bamberger & Co., of Munich. It was also marketed under the name of the manufacturer. The Berlin selling agent in 1907 was Richard Schwanke, Bernburgerstrasse 15-16, S. W.

Linowriter

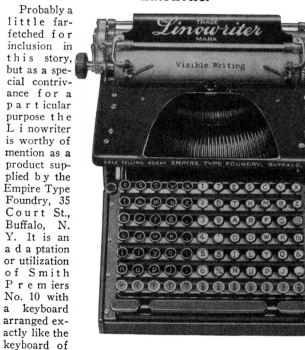

Probably a little farfetched for inclusion in this story, but as a special contrivance for a particular purpose the Linowriter is worthy of mention as a product supplied by the Empire Type Foundry, 35 Court St., Buffalo, N. Y. It is an adaptation or utilization of Smith Premiers No. 10 with a keyboard arranged exactly like the keyboard of the Linotype, the well-known type-setting machine, for use in typewriting without confusion by operators of the Linotype.

Long

In Charlottesville, Va., Eugene M. Long in 1906 invented a typewriter that could be carried in one's pocket.

Longini

Although not exactly a typewriter in the present acceptance of the term, the Longini of 1906 was a writing machine. It was not designed for correspondence, but intended instead for the writing of signs and placards in extra large letters by mechanical means. The machine wrote only capitals and the impression was accomplished through use of a large and upright type wheel. The card was slipped beneath, the wheel turned by means of a knob with the left hand and the printing done by pressure on a single key at the top. The Longini would write on paper, wood, cardboard or metal. It sold at a reasonable price and was manufactured by H. E. Longini, of Brussels, Belgium, now a leading office equipment dealer in that country. Even though not a typewriter in the popular sense, it can be said to be the first writing instrument made in Belgium.

Manhattan

This typewriter was very well known during its life, coming out in 1898 as the product of the Manhattan Typewriter Company of New York. In construction and appearance it was practically

identical with the Remington No. 2, though it had some features of its own. Expired patents were chiefly utilized in construction of the Manhattan and, as we say above, enjoyed a good market until overtaken by death-dealing difficulties. A revival of the enterprise was undertaken later by the Blake Typewriter Company of Newark, N. J., headed by Waldon Blake, but without success. Models of the Manhattan were designated by letters instead of the customary numbers.

M. A. P.

One of the new typewriter products of France, the M. A. P., is known to trade and users as such in initialed abbreviation of the name of its manufacturers, the famous Manufacture d'Armes

de Paris. It was designed by Halcolm Ellis, also inventor of the Ellis adding typewriter made in America. Nico Sanders is the managing director of the enterprise and to him is due chiefly the success attained.

The M. A. P. typewriter, which was placed on the market the middle of 1921, is a standard, single-shift, front-stroke machine possessing all usual modern features required by the buying public. It is built in two units, is backed by an impressive list of capitalists several of whom are on the board of directors and is already enjoying a wide and profitable sale. The name of the machine is derived from the initials of the manufacturing company's title.

The M. A. P. typewriter is very rapidly winning a commanding place in the industry, arrangements having been concluded in a number of important territories for adequate representation.

An outstanding instance is that for the British Isles, where W. Bateson is general sales manager with offices at 26-27, High Holborn, London, W. C. 1. The main offices of the makers, Manufacture d'Armes de Paris, are located at 6 Rue de Hanovre, Paris, France.

Manograph

Selling at $5.00 and weghing 2¼ Kg., the Manograph typewriter from somewhere in Europe made its appearance in 1906 designed principally for children's use.

Maskelyne

Differential spacing was the chief feature of the Maskelyne typewriter put on the market in 1889. It was visible writing, had double shift and, like many of its predecessors, had the carriage behind the typebars. In shift key manipulation, it was made optional with the purchaser whether he was supplied with or without a foot pedal for shifting purposes. England was the market for the most part, it being manufactured there. It was invented jointly by John Neville Maskelyne and his son, John Neville Maskelyne, Jr.

Megagraph

Not for commercial use, but for printing of newspaper bulletins and other similar matter, the Megagraph was made by one Mc-Cann. It stood six feet high, was five feet ten inches long and three feet four inches wide, a monster in its day among typewriters, weighing 400 pounds. It was more or less like standard machines of the commercial variety. How many were made we cannot say, but the manufacturer's price was $300 each.

Mentor

The typewriter product of the Metall-Industrie Schönebeck/Elbe, Germany, for which advantages are claimed in removable keyboard, carriage and platen. The advent of the Mentor No. 3, quite different from previous models, was an event calling for particular note.

Mercedes

This is one of the best known and most popular of German made typewriters. It was first made in 1907 by the Mercedes Bureau Maschinen Ges. m. b. H., Charlottenstr., Berlin, and was invented by Franz Schüller, who was one of the first typewriter engineers to command attention in Germany. Previous to joining the Mercedes enterprise, he had been for 15 years with Heinrich Kleyer. The factory is at Mehlis in Thuringen, to which location the general offices were moved in August, 1912, though now located in Berlin.

Various models of the Mercedes have been made, one of the most popular in ready acceptance by buyers being the No. 3 which came out first in December, 1911. Recently, in September, 1921, an electric model was added to the line, the machine being exactly like the regular product except for a slight addition along the side carrying the electric propelling mechanism for operation by such power.

The well-known leader in German typewriter affairs, Dr. Mez, is the moving spirit in promotion of Mercedes expansion.

Although the original Mercedes typewriter was invented by Mr. Schüller, the subsequent models are the creation of Carl Schlüns of Berlin. Mercedes machines have always been standard products with front-stroke typebars and the usually accepted requirements of the modern writing machine. Distinctive in the

THE ELECTRICALLY OPERATED MERCEDES TYPEWRITER

Mercedes is an adjustment to three different spacings between letters, permitting emphasis in writing, adaptation to long or short letters and completion of words on one line without continuation or abbreviation. The Mercedes also has an interchangeable type basket for multi-language writing.

Thoroughly high grade, single shift, 90 characters, two-color ribbon, back spacer, decimal tabulator, ball-bearing carriage, automatic ribbon reverse and interchangeable individual typebars is briefly descriptive of the Mercedes typewriter. The present standard Mercedes is Model 4. Although today known exclusively as the Mercedes, for a period in previous years it was sold in England as the Protos and in Argentine as the Cosmopolita. A post-war venture on the part of R. Parker Drake of London which never materialized intended assembling of the machine in England and its sale there as the Drake-London.

Mercury

Three models of the Mercury typewriter were made since its inception in 1899. The first was a double shift, typebar machine with semi-circular keyboard. The second had four rows, with 36 keys, and, like the first, wrote from a type wheel. Neither of these machines was manufactured, although a third model was produced for the market. The latter also employed a type wheel, had three rows of keys with a total of 30. The distinctive feature of the Mercury was the manner of writing. The operator depressed the key, the platen carrying the paper was automatically lifted against the type on the stationery type wheel and the inking was accomplished through use of an ink roll. This contribution to typewriter manufacture was invented by Frederick Myers of Liverpool and sold chiefly in England. The Mercury was a small machine retailing for less than £10.

Merritt

Another machine of the indicator type was the Merritt, containing 78 characters with a keyboard arranged on a two-row chart in front of the machine. Like in most others of its character, writing could be done only with the right hand, the left being required for moving the indicator to desired position. It came out in 1899 and was manufactured by the Lyon Manufacturing Company of New York City and retailed in the United States for $15.

Minimax

Similar to the Ideal in appearance, Berlin was the site picked for the manufacture of the Minimax type writer in 1907.

Meteor

The Meteor was first shown in April, 1911. It was a typebar machine made by the Sächsische Strickmaschinen-Fabik "Meteor" G. m. b. H., Dresden, Germany. It was a portable typewriter very

similar to the Standard Folding of American origination.

This machine in parts of Germany has also been known as the Forte-Type, but is not the previously mentioned Forte-Type which is a development of the older Faktotum. The similarity in adopted names is due to sale of both machines at different times as the Forte-Type by the same firm of Berlin distributors. The Pagina Fachhaus für Bürobedarf of Berlin have since 1922 been distributing their Pagina typewriter which is supposed to be identical with the Meteor.

Mignon

In 1904 this little machine was manufactured by the Union Schreibmaschinen G. m. b. H., understood to be the property of as a writing machine subsidiary of the Allgemeine Electrizitäts

Ges., Berlin, the largest concern in its field in Germany. The same interests are also making a standard typebar typewriter mentioned elsewhere and named the A.E.G.

The Mignon is a machine which departs generally from the so-called standard keyboard and typebar construction. It might be called an indicator type of machine, for on the left part there is a printed character table near which dangles a stylus or pointer which is used to manipulate the machine in printing of desired characters. A small bar, a sort of abbreviated space bar in appearance, is pressed down in printing, which is done through a ribbon from a long, cylindrical typewheel..

Mention of this little machine in 1908, when it is understood to have been priced at 100 Marks, indicated a good sale at that time. Especially during the World War was it broadly distributed, its interchangeable type wheel and the novelty of like change of the character chart making it quite popular. A very similar machine was the Yu Ess made by the Yu Ess Typewriter Co. of New York, but while the latter is no longer on the market the Mignon still enjoys a considerable sale. The main advantage of this machine, apart from the exceptionally cheap price, which is about one-third of the standard machine, is the large number of copies that can be typed, as well as the interchangeable letter table and type wheel on the same machine for different languages.

In order to greatly increase the output of the Mignon machine, as well as that of the standard A. E. G. typewriter made by tbhe same concern and described in its alphabetical order, the works in Erfurt, Germany, of the Deutsche Werke Aktiengesellschaft have been taken over by A. E. G. and the name of the manufacturers of the Mignon since the fusion is now A. E. G.-Deutsche

Werke Schreibmaschinen Gesellschaft m.b.H., Berlin, W. 66, Mauerstrasse 83/84.

Mimeograph

The A. B. Dick Company, makers of the duplicator of the same name, brought out what they called the Edison Mimeograph typewriter, placed on the market as "the outgrowth of an express demand for a typewriter to be used in connection with the Edison mimeograph for re-duplicating purposes," said the manufacturer. It was usable, also, for ordinary writing, in which case a ribbon was put on the machine. It was of the typebar kind, had a keyboard in the form of an arc of a circle, over which a pointer moved and when in place the impression made by use of the other hand. Besides the character pointer, three smaller pointers were set for capitals, small letters or figures. The machine weighed ten pounds and retailed at from $20 to $25. It disappeared from the market in about 1898.

Minerva

In 1912 a front stroke, standard sized machine called the Minerva was brought out by Karl Fr. Kührt, one of Germany's best known typewriter inventors whose products are not infrequently mentioned in this compilation. This machine is manufactured and distributed by Minerva Schreibmaschinen G.m.b.H., of Nürnberg, Germany. The Minerva is a single shift, 43 key machine selling at a very moderate price, several different and improved models having been manufactured since its inception. It is a thoroughly substantial machine for its exceedingly low price. Previous to the present name, it has also been known as the Rival, Mercurius, Regent, Lemco and Waterloo, as well as Kamo, Libra and Hacabo for several of its different models.

Model

In March, 1909, the Model Typewriter Company, Harrisburg, Penna., incorporated with capital stock of $150,000 subscribed by local interests, acquired a tract to erect a plant in that city to make a typewriter of the above name to sell at $60. The factory building was put up but never occupied, being sold at foreclosure in August, 1913. C. H. Bruder was president of the company. A machine to which the same name has been applied is now being perfected by R. W. Uhlig at his home in Allentown, Pa.

Molle

The first mention of the Molle Typewriter Company was the record of incorporation at $25,000 with the address of Antigo, Wis. In June, 1918, announcement was made of a model of the

machine being offered on the market known as the No. 3, a double shift typewriter weighing 11¾ pounds and priced at $50 retail. This was by the Molle Typewriter Company with factory at Oshkosh, Wis. On February 14, 1921, the stockholders of the company voted to increase the capitalization from $500,000 to $2,500,000. On July 3, 1922, the Molle Typewriter Corporation was adjudged bankrupt.

The Molle typewriter was designed by its inventor of the same name, a Wisconsin jeweler, to fill a demand for a machine between the portable and standard types. It had many of the usual modern features and considerable quantities were sold during the war, especially to countries outside of the United States. Because of substantial merit and proven durability, efforts at this writing are still being made to re-enliven the Molle company and machine.

Monarch

The Monarch upon its appearance in the year 1904 was regarded as a bold stroke in modern typewriter engineering. Many will remember its first public appearance at the Louisiana Exposition at St. Louis, where the late F. J. Tanner, whose identity with the Monarch Typewriter Company will also be recalled vividly, was in charge of the display. Another outstanding event in Monarch history was the move of the executive offices from the factory at Syracuse to New York, where on May 1, 1908, the company occupied the whole building at 300 Broadway.

EXTRA LONG CARRIAGES WERE ALWAYS AN OUTSTANDING CHARACTERISTIC OF MANY MONARCH TYPEWRITERS SOLD

The Monarch typewriter was successfully marketed for a number of years. The principal features of the Monarch were a light touch; ability to accelerate the movement of the type bars

and vary the touch by means of a set screw; a shifting segment, making the machine particularly adapted for the extra wide carriages; and an unobstructed view of the printing point.

E. E. Barney was with the Monarch Typewriter Company from its start in 1904 to 1909 in the capacity of Superintendent of Works at Syracuse, New York.

Moon-Hopkins

Although the present owners of the machine are an adding machine company and the product has long since been either regarded as a product foreign to the typewriter industry or was pushed so listlessly as to be almost forgotten, the Moon-Hopkins adding-typewriter is most emphatically worthy of a place in this narrative.

The merit of the product has never ceased to impress many members of the writing machine industry, and, though the Burroughs company now in control of the machine through purchase recently does not carry the word typewriter in their corporate title, that big and very well known Detroit institution is now very much in the typewriter business. For in the Moon-Hopkins machine there exists one of the most ingenious mechanisms in the world for combined type and figure writing with accompanying arithmetical calculations.

The Moon-Hopkins Billing Machine Co., St. Louis, Mo., first located at 19th and Pine Street and moved in 1911 to the corner of 22nd and O'Fallon streets was the original enterprise. It was on September 18, 1921, that the Burroughs Adding Machine Company acquired the valuable patents involved at a price said to be somewhere about $750,000.

The electrically fitted Moon-Hopkins machine makes one job of billing operations, writing and computing at the same time, and constitutes a contribution to development of the typewriter industry of distinguished prominence.

Monofix

In somewhat different and perhaps more improved form, the Monofix typewriter was introduced to the market in 1921 as the successor to the Mentor and is now manufactured by Bauchwitz-Pcherer A. G., of Leipzig, Germany.

Morris

This was another machine similar to the early Hall typewriter. It was manufactured by the Hoggson Manufacturing Company of New Haven, Conn., and invented by Robert Morris of Kansas City, Mo. It utilized a keyboard like the Hall, an indicator being moved to the proper position and the printing being done from a rubber plate. Of interest is the retail price of the Morris, namely, $15.

Moya

The accompanying illustration is of the writing in sight machine which was introduced in 1905, but the Moya was first brought out in 1902 as a non-visible machine. The first product had a

rubber type plate like the Hall, but was shortly succeeded by the machine which used a type cylinder like in the Crandall. The visible model had 28 keys, double shift, writing 84 characters, and universal keyboard. The machine of 1906 displayed some marked improvements, having a better type action and ribbon mechanism.

The inventors of the Moya were Hildago Moya, a Spanish-American whose identity with the writing machine industry is more prominently portrayed in the Imperial story appearing farther forward in this history, together with John G. Cathaway of Leicester, England. In the same city was located the plant of the manufacturers, The Moya Typewriter Company. The Moya was priced at five guineas.

Munson

This machine was first made in 1890 by the Munson Typewriter Manufacturing Company, but the plant, patents and other assets were bought in 1898 by Edgar A. Hill of Chicago, who continued its manufacture. It had a type-wheel, wrote through

a ribbon, had a universal keyboard, two shift-keys and weighed 16 pounds.

The type wheel or cylinder of this machine departed from the usual hard rubber composition, being made of metallic substance which brought durability. The writing was practically all visible and the type cylinders were interchangeable for different languages. Many of these typewriters were sold, an improved model making its appearance in 1897 which met with particularly good success. The Munson was invented by James Eugene Munson and Samuel John Siefried, the name being changed to the Chicago and the company to the Chicago Writing Machine Company. The enterprise was later moved from Chicago to Galesburg, Ill., at which time the name was again changed to the Galesburg typewriter, under which banner it disappeared from the market in about 1917.

This machine at different times was also sold as the Baltimore and as the Draper typewriter.

McCall

This was an automatic typewriter which wrote from a roll of paper attached to the machine, the invention of T. A. McCall. He was also president of the McCall Automatic Typewriter Company chartered in June, 1906, with capital stock of $500,000. The general offices and shop were first located at 218 and 220 North Fourth Street, Columbus, Ohio. A year later mention was made of the plant being located at Xenia, Ohio.

McCool

The Acme-Keystone Manufacturing Company, with sales offices in Pittsburgh and factory at Beaver Falls, Pa., had something to do with a typewriter of this name. It was a machine of 319 parts, wrote from a type wheel and was priced at $25 in anticipation of creating popular and broad demand through low price. There was such a typewriter and it was also quite certainly being made ready for the market, but nothing came of the effort. William W. McCool was the inventor.

National (I)

To identify this earlier product of the same name as differing from that following in the next paragraph, we call this

National (I), the invention of Henry Harmon Unz. It was a comparatively low priced machine of three banks, double shift, 81 characters, type-bar pattern appearing in 1889. The National (I) was a blind writer, necessitating raising of the carriage for inspection of the work, was priced at $60 and was manufactured by the National Typewriter Company of Philadelphia, Pa.

National

As this machine is at present more or less upon the market, it is given the title without suffix. There was also use of the word by the National Automatic Typewriter Company, but as that enterprise was merged with another in 1912, we are still able to apply this designation to the little portable here illustrated. It is a double shift, three bank, front stroke, ribbon writing machine with a retail price upon it when last offered under this name of $57. It was later known as the Portex.

The No. 2 National typewriter manufactured by the Rex Typewriter Corporation for a period in 1919 sold in Switzerland through their representative there as the Express.

First, in December, 1917, this machine was sold by the National

Typewriter Department of the Rex Typewriter Company. The National No. 3 was announced in January, 1918, at which time the sale of Rex Typewriter Company products in the United States and Canada was taken over by the American Can Company with Ben Harris as general sales manager of the division created for marketing of office devices. Marketing was later returned to the Rex Typewriter Company and in January, 1920, the Model 5 National was put out as an offering of the National Typewriter Company of Fond du Lac, Wisconsin.

New Century

This machine was actually named the New Century Caligraph, offered as an improvement over the former Caligraph. But it was such a radical change as compared with the older machine that it

lost, at least so far as designating title among typewriter men was concerned, its predecessor's name. About the only similarity with the old Caligraph was the double keyboard of the New Century, but even this was different because of the adoption in the newer product of the universal arrangement which the former did not have. It had a ball-bearing carriage and much shortened typebar. The first New Century in 1900 was the No. 6. Manufacture of the New Century ceased in 1906. It was one of the products of the famous Union Typewriter Company of America and was marketed by the American Writing Machine Company. Walter J. Barron, who died about two years ago, was the inventor of the New Century.

New England

A slow writing machine, utilizing a type wheel for printing, the New England typewriter was of English origin. It dropped from the market shortly after its appearance in 1907.

Niagara

An indicator type of machine called the Niagara displayed some difference from many others of similar kind in the fact that a circular scale or chart with the alphabet imprinted thereon for service in correspondence to the keyboard of bar typewriters stood upright in front of the machine. A knob in the center of the scale served for manipulation of the indicator and the printing was done by means of a type wheel on a regular hard rubber platen.

The Niagara was put out in 1905 by the Blickensderfer Manufacturing Company, Stamford, Conn., to fill a demand for a low priced machine where speed was of minor importance. It retailed at $15.

Nickerson

C. S. Nickerson, a Presbyterian minister, was the inventor of a typewriter which was known in its struggle to get on the market by the same name as its hopeful sponsor. He was also the president of the Nickerson Typewriter Company, by whom was established a tool-making shop at 30-32 South Canal Street, Chicago, in March, 1907, in preparation for manufacture. But the Nickerson typewriter never reached the marketable stage. It had a large cylinder platen which stood upright and, in like man-

ner to its contradiction in position to others, wrote the short way around the platen instead of across. Its chief claim was the shorter and quicker return to the starting of lines by the one revolution of the platen, undoubtedly the most radical departure in construction known to the typewriter industry.

Noiseless

The Noiseless typewriter had its origin in an association between W. P. Kidder of Jamaica Plain, Mass., and C. C. Colby of Stanstead, Quebec, Canada—an association which, beginning in 1891, covered many years and was marked by close, personal friendship. Mr. Kidder had already won a wide reputation as an inventor of printing presses, and he had also invented two typewriters, the Franklin and the Wellington. At the time when he and Mr. Colby first met, arrangements were being made to build and market the Wellington typewriter, of which the distinguishing feature was a sliding typebar functioning through a direct thrust. Mr. Colby undertook to establish the manufacture and sale of this machine throughout the British Empire as well as on the Continent of Europe. With the manufacture and sale of the Wellington in the United States he had no connection.

For several years following 1891, Mr. Colby devoted much attention to the interests of the Wellington typewriter in countries outside of the United States. He first organized The Imperial Writing Machine Company which built the Wellington machine in Canada under the name of "The Empire," and sold it throughout the British Empire. He also created a company with headquarters at Brussels which sold the Empire in the western part of Europe. For Germany and eastern countries he effected an arrangement on a royalty basis with the Adler Company, whose works are at Frankfort-on-Main. As a result of these activities Mr. Colby became deeply interested in the whole subject of typewriter construction, with particular reference to improving the design of the writing machine past a point which had been reached twenty-five years ago. Simultaneously Mr. Kidder was considering the mechanical problems involved in producing a typewriter which would function without noise. At a conference held toward the close of 1896 it was decided by these associates that in order to give the typewriter its full development and usefulness, the unpleasant, distracting clatter of the machine must be got rid of. According to Mr. Kidder's original conception, this could only be done effectively and permanently through the invention of a type action which would function by pressure rather than by hammering. Mr. Colby, having agreed to furnish financial support and business counsel, the long effort began.

From 1896 to 1904 the Noiseless typewriter was an idea beginning to take concrete form. During this period Mr. Kidder

THE LATEST NOISELESS, THE No. 5 NINETY-CHARACTER MACHINE INTRODUCED LAST MONTH

produced several models of a pressure printing machine which had its structural basis in toggle-cam action. While these showed steady progress it became clear that the mechanical difficulties involved were such as to make a heavy demand upon both time and money. In 1904 the effort was placed upon a wider basis through the organization of the Parker Machine Company, which was created for the purpose of bringing the Kidder model of the Noiseless typewriter to a point where it would be ready to manufacture.

The headquarters of the Parker Machine Company were in

Buffalo, owing to the fact that that city was the residence of several gentlemen who became associated with Mr. Kidder and Mr. Colby in carrying on the task of perfecting the Noiseless. This connection was brought about through the friendship of Mr. Kidder and G. E. Matthews, president of the Matthews Northrup Company, which owned and published the *Buffalo Express.* Mr. Matthews, in turn, enlisted the aid of W. Caryl Ely, then one of the leading lawyers and financiers of western New York. Mr. Kidder and Mr. Colby were among the leading shareholders of the Parker Machine Company, which, in the aggregate, expended about $500,000 in developing the Noiseless typewriter, during the years 1904-1909. Though a New York corporation, the Parker Machine Company carried on its experimental work at Woonsocket, R. I., and Hartford, Connecticut. In order to perfect a typewriter that would admit of volume production by means of machinery and special tools, a board of engineers and draughtsmen was organized with a membership which included W. P. Kidder, C. W. Sponsel, W. A. Lorenz, J. A. Ronchetti, E. L. Clark, N. H. Anderson, E. Bishop and several others.

The fact should be emphasized that down to 1908 the Parker Machine Company had acquired no factory nor had it provided any working capital for manufacturing the Noiseless typewriter. The large expenditures made prior to this date had gone to develop the pressure printing typewriter to a point where it seemed a thoroughly commercial product. In 1908 the goal appeared to

THE NOISELESS PORTABLE AND ITS CARRYING CASE

have been reached, so far as a solution of the mechanical problems was concerned. It remained to build the Noiseless typewriter and put it on the market. At this stage the Parker Machine Company became the Silent Writing Machine Company by a recapitalization and exchange of securities—the Silent Writing Machine Company being incorporated in the State of New York. There was no sale of securities to outside parties in connection with the transfer of patents or other property. The Silent Writing Machine Company was the Parker Machine Company with a new name and an enlarged capitalization, all the shareholders of the one company becoming ipso facto shareholders of the other.

The Silent Writing Machine Company had for its essential purpose the creation of an organization by which the Noiseless typewriter could be manufactured and sold throughout the world on a scale that harmonized with the importance of the invention. Here the central idea was to procure manufacture in the United States, in Great Britain and in Germany. The directors of the Silent Writing Machine Company—all of whom had been actively engaged in developing the Noiseless typewriter during the period of the Parker Machine Company—were men of high standing, who had strong financial connections. Their belief in the future of the Noiseless typewriter was such that they did not shrink from the responsibility of embarking their own capital in an enterprise conceived of on large lines, nor from embarking their credit through the sale of securities to their own friends.

The first step was to begin manufacture in the United States, and during the Autumn of 1908 the Silent Writing Machine Company entered upon a negotiation for the purchase of a large factory at Middletown, Conn., being the same factory which is owned and operated by the present Noiseless Typewriter Company.

Having completed the contract for the purchase of the property on the 31st day of December, 1908, the Silent Writing Machine Company proceeded forthwith to organize the Noiseless Typewriter Company of Connecticut—a corporation which, in turn

for a portion of its securities, was given the right to manufacture and sell Noiseless typewriters throughout the Western Hemisphere.

The president of the first Noiseless Typewriter Company was the late W. Caryl Ely, who worked with the utmost devotion and determination to overcome inherently insuperable obstacles, and whose memory occupies a foremost place in the annals of the Noiseless typewriter. The first president of the present Noiseless Typewriter Company was Joseph Merriam, of Middletown, Connecticut, who had been one of the most active, useful members of the first company, and whose assistance at the moment of reorganization had proved most valuable. J. A. Ruffin was made works manager, and E. J. Sheehan, sales manager.

Cyrus Field failed in his first effort to lay the Atlantic cable. The first effort to place a noiseless typewriter on the market was also unsuccessful. None the less both enterprises went forward.

To explain in full detail why misfortune overtook the company which attempted to build and sell the cam machine would be to tell a long story—a story made up of courage, perseverance and good faith contending against inherent difficulties which were only disclosed as manufacture went forward and the product was actually placed before the public. It is impossible within present limits to describe all the factors which entered into the problem.

However, out of all the toil and trouble which marked the efforts of the first Noiseless Typewriter Company, there came one solid result. In 1912, N. H. Anderson, one of the company's engineers, invented a type action which rendered it possible to eliminate cams wholly from the machine, at the same time accelerating the speed very greatly and lightening the touch to a marked degree. This invention, which centers in double toggle, or momentum accumulator action at once cured the difficulties which had been caused by the cams. During the course of 1912 enough of these new machines were produced to make it clear that the double toggle structure did indeed provide a remedy for the troubles before encountered. The next step was to bring this new machine to the market.

During the nine months from June, 1914, to March, 1915, tools for the new machine were in process of construction, and during the remaining nine months of 1915, the new product was being tested out carefully in small quantities. In fact, less than five hundred machines were sold during 1915. In 1916 a considerably larger product was marketed but no real effort was made to crowd sales, it being the policy of the Board to make sure that the machine was right before trying to sell it in a large way. As a result of the experience gained during 1915 and 1916, a new model was brought out at the beginning of 1917—the No. 4 model which represents the Noiseless typewriter in its first fully commercial and satisfactory form. This machine, which is based upon double toggle action as refined and developed by the experimental department during 1915 and 1916, has brought the Noiseless Typewriter Company to the point which it has now reached. Much credit for improvement in design during the period of the present company is due to G. G. Going, the chief engineer. Of late Mr. Going's attention has been largely occupied with the development of the Portable Noiseless, which came out in November, 1921, and then described in these columns. The latest product, the No. 5 90-character Noiseless, was announced only last month.

This new Noiseless machine contains 90 characters and is designed to fill the requirement not only where special characters are necessary but carries with it a particular appeal in those countries where language specifications demand more than the usual 84. It has a bi-chrome ribbon and although practically the same in appearance as the regular Noiseless model, the arrangement of its 90 characters give it a standard, universal keyboard.

For some time past the president of the company has been Dr. C. W. Colby, and in August, 1921, the organization was greatly strengthened by the addition of A. F. Hebard, as vice-president.

Nordisk

In September, 1918, mention was first made of the Nordisk typewriter being promoted by Nordisk Skrivemaskinefabrik, of Copenhagen, Denmark. The enterprise promised to develop into a reality, a model of the machine having been built and a factory partially equipped for manufacture at the time mentioned, but since that time there has been no further indication of successful outcome of plans for manufacture of this machine as a Danish contribution to the typewriter industry.

Norica

While a hand made model was shown in 1905, the Norica typewriter as a commercial product was first made ready for the market in 1907. It is understood to have been manufactured by

Deutsche Triumph-Fahrradwerke A.-G., Nuremberg, Germany, or at least by interests very close to the enterprise named, who, in 1910, were sponsors for a writing machine product referred to elsewhere as the Triumph. Kührt & Riegelman G.m.b.H., of the same city, were also referred to in the early days of the Norica as selling representatives in offering of the machine at a price corresponding to $90 in American money value. A new model was launched in 1908 and another in March, 1910. The Norica was a single shift, four bank, visible writing machine in many respects of standard construction. Its typebars in normal position at an approximate angle of 45° was a compromise between the Columbia Bar-Lock and the Underwood. Carl F. Kührt was the inventor.

North

This typewriter has been broadly illustrated and referred to by narrators chiefly attracted by novelty in design, for in the North the typebars stood perpendicularly behind the platen and

struck forward and downward from a position comparatively far above the keyboard. It was, consequently, an almost totally visible writing machine, the platen being between the keyboard and the typebars.

The bars on the North, which was born in 1892, were arranged in two semi-circles, the outside row standing higher than the inner. It was a four row, single shift machine writing 76 characters. Its manifolding qualities were good and it had a ball bearing carriage. In reality, the North was the older English typewriter with improvements, this, like the English, being invented by George B. Cooper and Morgan Dunne. It got its name from Lord North, a wealthy member of England's nobility who had enormous South American holdings and financed the project. The machine would perhaps have enjoyed a longer and much greater success were it not for Lord North's sudden death. As it was, the North was sold only in England and France, the manufacturing company being the North Typewriter Manufacturing Co., Ltd., of London.

Odell

The chief claim made by the manufacturers of the Odell typewriter was that it cost only one-fifth the price of standard typewriters, probably another instance of misguided judgment which

was responsible for efforts to sell machines because of price. It was of the ink pad kind of machine, had 78 characters in two rows of keys and two shifts. Spacing was done with the left hand and all the writing with the right, the method being by use of an indicator moved to required point. The Odell weighed eight pounds and was priced at $20.

Odoma

One of Germany's more recent of the large number of new typewriter undertakings in that country is the Odoma, first known as the Odo but since changed to the name of the heading. This

machine appeared in 1921 as the finished product of the Odo Maschinenfabrik G.m.b.H. of Darmstadt and is a 45 key, single shift machine of attractive design, easy action and modern construction and features. The main features of the Odoma are very quiet running, automatic ribbon reverse, ball bearing carriage, and all other first-class attachments and improvements are fixed on the Odoma typewriter. The carriage, platen, typebar and type can easily be removed and replaced. The machine is also supplied with two exchangeable carriages.

The Odoma typewriter has been upon the market two and a half years and has met with approval in many countries. The enterprise has recently moved into their own factory building which is provided with their own steam pressure machinery and the most modern tool machines; and the capacity of this factory meets every requirement. The manufacturers give special attention to first-class material and first-class workmanship.

Official

A type wheel machine of partially visible writing which relied upon a ribbon in its printing was the Official of 1901. It had a three row keyboard and in all contained only 170 parts. It was invented by Charles E. Peterson of Brooklyn, New York, and R. C. Cox of New York City, the machine for a while having been manufactured in the American metropolis.

Oliver

At a convention banquet on December 31, 1902, held by the Oliver Typewriter Company in Chicago, Thomas Oliver, inventor of the Oliver typewriter, told of his early inventive proclivities

and his decision to make a typewriter of his own for use in his work; he was a minister. Lack of space alone prevents reprinting of his address in this issue, but it most surely will be used later in further detailed reference to the struggles of the Reverend Oliver from the start of his experiments in 1888. Just ten years prior to the convention date mentioned above, the birth of the Oliver typewriter took place when in the year 1892 the crude model of the first Oliver typewriter was patented.

In December, 1894, the first Oliver that actually brought money to the treasury of the company selling the Oliver was sold—

Model No. 1, Serial number 3. It is a coincidence that the man to whom the first Oliver typewriter was sold was a professional man, also a minister of the gospel. This machine foretold the durability that in later years was to be so widely known. It is a matter of record that this particular machine remained in service and received hard use for over ten years before the owner was willing to exchange it for a later model of the Oliver typewriter.

The present corporation started business in the fall of the year 1895, with offices occupying two small rooms on the ninth floor of the building located on the northeast corner of Clark and Randolph Streets, Chicago, Ill., from which in May, 1896, it became necessary to move into larger quarters, and a part of the sixth floor of the building at the northwest corner of Clark and Madison streets was rented. Here the Oliver began to make itself known, and by May, 1898, the business had developed to such an extent that another move was forced upon the company. The large banking offices at the northeast corner of Dearborn and Washington streets were rented and handsomely fitted and furnished. It then seemed as though the company had established a location for all time, but February of 1900, less than two years after taking possession of those handsome and well-located quarters, the company was driven out by lack of room to handle its business properly and compelled to make another move.

This time it was decided to make no mistake—thirty-six employees, together with heads of departments, were transferred to the spacious ground floor location at 107-109 Lake Street, where

The Most Recent of Oliver Typewriters, the Model 11 "Speedster"

13,200 square feet of floor space was made available for the company's use. Less than two and a half years later that room could not accommodate the departments and take care of the ever-increasing business to the company's satisfaction. After careful deliberations on the part of the Board of Directors, quarters commensurate with the size and importance of the company, and with due consideration for its undoubted growth, were secured at the southeast corner of Wabash Avenue and Monroe Street, the whole second floor, 80x171 feet, being devoted to the general offices of the company. Immediately under these spacious quarters the Chicago branch office with a frontage of 40 feet on Wabash Avenue, one of the most important thoroughfares in the city of Chicago, with ample facilities for storage and repair rooms in the basement, was located.

However, in but a few years more the company had outgrown these spacious quarters and it was decided to erect their own building. With the completion of their building at 159 to 167 North Dearborn Street, the present home of the Oliver was occupied in June, 1907. But the original building, which was five stories, was in later years added to in order to accommodate the increased amount of business.

The growth of the factory in this time can well be imagined and today the Oliver factory, located at Woodstock, Ill., where the first factory building of the present corporation was erected, is one of the finest of its kind in the world.

A sorrowful note in Oliver history was the death on January 16, 1920, of Lawrence Williams, many years the company's president. In this resumé can also be recorded the passing of William T. Harding, long general manager of the Oliver Typewriter Co.,

Ltd., of London. Otherwise, for the most part, executives in direction of Oliver activities are much the same as for a long period, the old timer, John Whitworth, still being in full charge of production at the manufacturing plant. Henry Kidder Gilbert succeeded the late Lawrence Williams as president and the son of the latter bearing the same name is at present the manager of agencies and a shareholder in the Oliver company by inheritance from his father. Fred W. Walker is now the president.

On October 30, 1894, the Model No. 2 Oliver, the first machine to be manufactured by the present corporation was patented. This was followed by the Model No. 3 Oliver on March 1, 1898,

from which dates the reputation accorded the Oliver typewriter. In succesive order the following models were produced—May, 1907—Model No. 5. January, 1915—Model No. 7. March, 1916—Model No. 9.

And out of the ripe experiences of the years since 1892 and the big plant at Woodstock, Ill., came in July, 1922, the latest Oliver, the Model 11, called the "Speedster." It is a type writer of today, but its principles are deep rooted in the practical vision of Thomas Oliver.

Olivetti

Most everybody in the industry would unquestionably grant to the Olivetti typewriter the distinction of being the first ever made in Italy, which, of course, it is in an industrial way, yet

Mr. Olivetti himself is most insistent that the machine of Giuseppe Ravizza, invented over 70 years ago, should be given the proud honor of having been the first Italian typewriter. In fact, we are indebted to Mr. Olivetti for details regarding the early invention appearing among machines of ancient classification as the ancestral predecessor of his machine.

But, as we say above, the original typewriter of Italian inventi n first industrially produced in that country was the Olivetti, a worthy contribution to writing machine history of standard provision as to features and quality. It was developed in the years 1909 to 1910 under original Italian patents dated April 4, 1909, and May 24, 1910, and U. S. patent dated May 23, 1911, numerous other Italian and foreign patents covering later improvements and additions. Ing. C. Olivetti & Co., Ivrea, Italy, manufacture the Olivetti, a fully original machine in mechanical movements very simple, an escapement entirely on ball bearings which is rapid and strong and in all details of utmost ingenuity.

The factory facilities for manufacture of the Olivetti at Ivrea, Italy, furnish a subject for historical comment. The original building was designed and constructed in 1895 by Mr. Olivetti for production of electric measuring instruments. That factory was afterwards transferred to Milan, and from there to Monza, but when Mr. Olivetti started to work on a typewriter in 1908 he used the original building in Ivrea, the first example in Italy of reinforced concrete construction. The plant has, of course, been greatly enlarged in recent years and is thoroughly modern in every particular.

The decimal tabulator of the Olivetti is a particularly practical feature. The location of the plant in the same district where the famous Italian motor cars are made provides mechanics highly proficient in metal finishing; hence the finish of the Olivetti. The width of the writing line, 9¼ inches giving 90 characters to the line, is in its favor. Other features are the quick and powerful stroke, speedy change of platen, an excellent card holder, a very light carriage of pressed steel, an efficient marginal stop and all standard requirements.

The Olivetti policy is to develop a sound business in few countries where the product can be appreciated, and not to scatter few machines everywhere. Besides Italy, where they have branch houses and agents in the whole country, they have done good work in Belgium, Argentina Republic, Egypt and Holland, and a few other countries. The result is that all the output of the factory, which is naturally not as large as many other concerns, is oversold; this is the only reason why the Olivetti people have not endeavored hitherto to push their commercial organization further afield, but the Olivetti nevertheless is a typewriter product which is destined to occupy a highly important place in the industry reviewed in this historical compilation.

Orga

The Orga typewriter is a 44 key, shift key machine of very modern construction and composed of features that speak well for a promising future. It appeared on the market in 1922 and is a standard office machine with semi-circular segment, typebars, removable carriage and platen and all the usual requirements expected in writing machines of today. The removable carriage of the Orga permits ready accessibility for cleaning. This machine is a product of the famous Bing Works of Nürnberg, Germany, known the world over for their toys. They are achieving success with their new typewriter and are gradually extending their export activities to the extent that even the United States may be entered through their New York branch affiliations, Jno. Bing & Company.

Otto

Another instance of invention of a writing instrument by a minister is the Otto. Patents were issued in 1907 to Rev. H. J. Otto, of Princeton, Ind., for a pneumatically operated machine, his plan including the installation of air pumps in the basements of office buildings where large numbers of his typewriters would be in use for supply of air power, a mere touch being required to manipulate the keys and the driving force coming from a source much like the supply of electric light, telephone, etc. It is no reflection against the ambitions of this inventor to say that he was many years ahead of the times in his vision, but who will say that something of the kind will not mark the coming like number of years which are celebrated in retrospect by this 50th anniversary number?

Parisienne

A low priced indicator machine with the so-called keyboard arranged in a circle with indicator secured in center and revolving entirely around the dial like front. When the indicator was depressed at a certain letter, the machine printed direct from rubber type on paper beneath, ink being applied by two ink rolls. The Parisienne wrote only capital letters and was the invention of Ernest Enjalbert of Paris, France.

Parker

Roy D. Parker, of Goshen, Indiana, invented an automatic typewriter in 1906 which he claimed would be a great time saver over the machines then in use, it being possible to write an entire page without touching the carriage. It was said at the time that the machine had been carefully patented and that a company would be organized to manufacture it.

Patria

Experimental work for two years by "Vulcan" Maschinenfabrik-Actien-Gesellschaft, Vienna, Austria, resulted in building of models for the Patria typewriter, but it was never put onto the market.

Peerless

The birth of the Peerless typewriter was in 1891, a full keyboard machine with a key for each of its 76 characters that re-sembled the Smith Premier. It was one of the invisible writers on which the carriage had to be raised to read what was written. The manufacturers were the Peerless Typewriter Company of Ithaca, New York, in which at the time Dwight McIntyre, L. H. Smith, George Livermore, James McNamara and C. M. Clinton were interested. During the rather brief life of the Peerless it sold at retail at $97.50.

People's

The well known and long existing Garvin Machine Company of New York City, now located at the corner of Spring and Varick Streets, were the manufacturers for its owners of the Peoples typewriter, also sold under the name of the Pearl, in 1893. It was a simple indicator type of machine utilizing a type wheel for printing. The indicator was moved to the desired letter or figure with the right hand and with the left hand a key was depressed that brought the wheel sharply around and against the paper.

Perfection

Invention by Richard W. Uhlig in 1906 of the Perfection typewriter included a type bar movement which was novel.

Perkeo

The writing machine manufacturing enterprise of Clemens Müller G. m. b. H., of Dresden, Germany, referred to later in this condensed history as makers of the Urania, a standard machine,

also produce a small portable typewriter known as the Perkeo. Its design and features are not unlike the former Standard Folding made in America, being light in weight and easily carried in a traveling case.

The Perkeo was formerly known as the Albus and was made in Vienna, Austria, but when bought by Clemens Müller it was improved and strengthened and renamed the Perkeo. In France this same portable typewriter was for a while sold as the Galliette, and for a short period, starting in 1910, it was sold in Germany as the Emka, this name being given to it by Max Keller, general agent in Germany for the Albus at the time it was being manufactured in Vienna.

Phoenix

Appearing in 1908 and manufactured by the Ges. f. Apparate & Maschinenbau G. m. b. H., of Berlin, Germany, the Phoenix typewriter, the same as the previously appearing Merkur of which very few were made, was a simple and crude mechanism of double shift and printing typewheel designed to sell at the exceedingly low price of less than $25. Although manufacture has ceased, several models of the Phoenix were produced.

A small machine without typebars and selling at a low price, a German product belonging to the toy class was sold for a short time many years ago as the Phönix, this reference being included here for the reason that the spelling is different from that in the heading, though it is very likely that the historical data responsible for the latter listing refers to the former more completely chronicled machine.

Picht

A typewriter of this name for use by the blind was first exhibited at an office equipment show in Venice, Italy, in 1907, though it had been invented in 1899 by Oscar Picht, director of the Institute for the Blind in Eberswalde, Germany. It was manufactured by Von Herde & Wendt, Sebastianstr. 72, Berlin, Germany.

The Picht machine was made with two keyboards, one for operation with both hands and one when use of the right hand alone was desired. The Braille alphabet for the blind with its well known dot system was employed. The machine could handle not only the standard Braille abbreviated alphabet but in capitals all the regular letters of the ordinary Roman alphabet for the benefit of those who had not mastered the Braille system.

Pittsburgh

An improvement over the formerly named Daugherty typewriter was called the Pittsburgh Visible, the first under this title being in 1898. It was manufactured by the Pittsburgh Writing Machine Company of Kittaning, Pa.

The Pittsburgh Visible had an interchangeable type basket, permitting the use of different keyboards and languages on the same machine. An interchangeable and removable carriage was also a feature. Several different models were made, chiefly designed to make the functioning mechanism removable and interchangeable, this provision finally being extended to include the keyboard, ribbon mechanism, etc. In all, 12 different models were made, the product known as the Reliance of later day being a practical and improved form of this evolution.

A receiver was appointed for the Pittsburgh Visible Typewriter Company and the Pittsburgh Writing Machine Company in July, 1913. The plant at Kittaning, Pa., was sold on March 16, 1914, for $12,000 to J. S. Kuhn of Pittsburgh.

Polygraph

A machine called the Polygraph was made by the Polyphon Musikwerke Act. G., Aktiengesellschaft, in Wahren, near Leipzig, and sold at 300 marks in its day. It first appeared in 1903.

Typebars which stood upright and striking backward on an underlying platen, as in the older Bar-Lock and Salter, with a keyboard which had the extreme capacity of 103 characters printable from 34 keys and two shift keys is descriptive of the Polygraph. The keys and keyboard arrangement were similar to the original Ideal Hammond in the first models, but in 1906 the machine as illustrated with universal keyboard in straight rows replaced the earlier semi-circular arrangement. From first to last, however, the Polygraph, upon which manufacture ceased in 1909, retained the double shift with three rows of keys and the large character capacity.

Postal

This is a typewriter of the portable family which dates back to 1902, when the Postal Typewriter Company was incorporated in New York. The first factory was at 45 Cliff Street, near Fulton Street, but in

May, 1904, the manufacturing equipment was moved to a property on Knight Street at Norwalk, Conn., where also the general offices were taken.

The Postal enterprise prospered and in April, 1906, the company purchased the building which they

had formerly occupied as a tenant. At one time 2,000 agents in the United States alone sold Postal typewriters. A type wheel machine, much like the Blickensderfer, it sold first at $25 but later on at from $30 to $35, the No. 7 Postal introduced in 1908 being priced at $50. The president and treasurer of the Postal Typewriter Company and the prime driving force in the company was N. L. Carpenter. The inventors of the Postal were William P. Quentell and Franklin Judge.

Portex

When the Rex Typewriter Company re-assumed the National Typewriter Company in May, 1922, they renamed the portable typewriter formerly known as the National. In a combination of

"portable" and "Rex," Portex was evolved and at the same time the machine was reduced in weight to 9 pounds. It is a front-stroke, double-shift portable typewriter with which the trade is more or less intimately familiar because of its recentness.

Presto

The portable typewriter now called Presto is different from the Presto machine referred to under the Senta heading, although the present Presto distributing personnel is identical with the earlier selling staff. The newer machine appeared on the market about two years ago and is a double-shift ,90-character machine. It has the usual necessary features and is the object of production by the Presto Bureaumaschinenbau, G.m.b.H., of Dresden, Germany.

Proctor

A standard, front-stroke typewriter bearing the name of Proctor, with various high-grade features in construction and operation, has been in the course of preparation for the market these past few years. It is not yet definitely known just when it will officially appear publicly but it can be said that it is the product of a well-known Baltimore, Md., manufacturer and that it is the invention of A. F. Mulhare.

Progress

Making its appearance in 1921, the Progress typewriter bearing a very close resemblance to the previously appearing Reliable machine is manufactured in the typewriter works attached to the plant of Hugo Kührt in Nürnberg, Germany. It is made for exclusive sale under the Progress name by Partsch & Fabian of Leipzig. The same machine has also been sold as the Liga.

Protos

The accompanying illustration, while small, gives an idea of the Protos typewriter manufactured by Zimmer & Co., Schreibmaschinenfabrik, Frankfurt a.M., Hanauerlandstrasse 165/67. It is distributed in Germany and German Austria by Bürotechnische Gesellschaft m .b. H., München.

The firm of Zimmer & Co. have for the past two years been manufacturing and marketing their Protos typewriter, a machine of the well-known forward thrust typebar action. The machine has all the requirements of the modern typewriter built into it and it is thoroughly durable, easy writing and efficient. The bar action is rapid and quiet, the carriage and platen removable and all parts of the machine readily accessible for cleaning. The keyboard is of 30 keys and 90 characters. The writing is clear and visible, excellent manifolding possibilities being a strong feature. The Protos is adopted to all languages and keyboards. The manufacturers put particular emphasis upon the mechanism which preserves a permanent alignment.

Pocket

As its name would indicate, this was a small typewriter capable of being stored away in the pocket. The Pocket was first made in 1894, a small, toy-like writing mechanism selling in the United States for $2. It was too simple in construction to be of utility for commercial purposes.

Prouty

A reproduction of a drawing, in like manner to others appearing earlier in this abbreviated history of the writing machine, must suffice for the Prouty typewriter, visible writing except im-

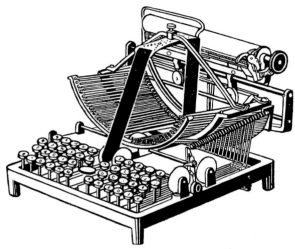

THIS SKETCH OF THE PROUTY TYPEWRITER IS FROM THE COLLECTION OF ILLUSTRATIONS OWNED BY C. V. ODEN

mediately behind the ribbon at the printing point, the invention in 1888 of E. Prouty of Chicago, Ill.

The first evidence of a modern front-strike typewriting machine came with the almost simultaneous inventions of this and the Grundy patent mentioned elsewhere, says E. B. Hess, of the Royal Typewriter Company, in his observations compiled into book form. With the typebars pivotally mounted in a circle in a vertically arranged segment below the printing point, the typebars lying in a substantially horizontal position and adopted to be moved to the printing point above, presenting a full face type impression for each and every one of the typebars, irrespective of the position in which it is mounted in the segment, is the language of Mr. Hess in further description of the Prouty machine. The necessary new arrangement of ribbon feeding mechanism for this type of machine and the vertical shifting of the platen are likewise spoken of as noteworthy accomplishments.

Rapid

The Rapid without prefix in 1890 and the New Rapid in 1892 might be divided into two subjects, though one description practically covers

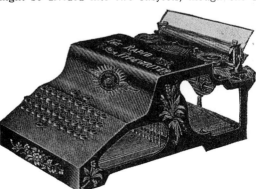

both. This machine had 84 characters, being a 42-key product with one shift, and differed in construction from previous typewriters. Instead of the tyebars striking up like on the Remington of that day or down as on the Bar Lock, the action of the bars on the

Rapid was forward along the lines of the Empire and Adler. The carriage and platen were behind the typebars. Writing was performed through a ribbon. The Rapid was invented by Bernard Granville and manufactured by A. W. Gump & Company at Dayton, Ohio.

Regina

Shilling & Krämer, of Suhl i. Thüringen, Germany, put the Regina typewriter out in 1904, although the partnership was established back in 1863 for operation of an iron foundry. As re-

cently as the September number of this international trade paper, a new model of the Regina typewriter was announced as Model VII. The Regina is a development from the older Germania Visible typewriter which was manufactured in the factory of the Jewett Typewriter Company in Des Moines, Iowa, and assembled in Germany by the firm of J. Scheffer-Hoppenhoefer, of Sundern. They improved the product and turned it over to the present manufacturers, Schilling & Krämer of Suhl in Thuringen, Germany.

One of Germany's standard typewriters today, the Regina is enjoying a substantial export sale. It is a front stroke, single shift machine of 42 characters. It has all the modern features as well as several distinctively its own. One feature permits cleaning of the machine by movement of the carriage to the extreme right and ready raising thereof to obtain complete accessibility to the interior, similar, as some of our readers will remember, to the construction of F. W. Hillard's special Underwood carriage.

Remington

The history of the Remington typewriter is a complete covering of the 50 years since the birth of the typewriter industry which has its semi-centennial trade paper celebration in the compilation

THE SHOLES AND GLIDDEN MACHINE WITH WHICH THE REMINGTONS WERE INDUCED TO TAKE UP THE MANUFACTURE OF TYPEWRITERS IN 1873

of which this is a part. What led up to the undertaking of E, Remington & Sons, the gun makers of Ilion, New York, to manufacture a typewriter has been told in detail; the early efforts starting in the year 1867 when Christopher Latham Sholes first conceived the idea of a "type-writer" and subsequent submission of the model here illustrated are now familiar to all members of the trade.

In 1816, Eliphalet Remington, at the forge of his father, who was a blacksmith at Ilion, made a gun for his own use. Then he made guns for others, finally creating a gun factory. Large output and wide reputation for Remington guns and other products was developed by three sons. Philo, the elder brother, was the president and head of the business when, in February, 1873, James Densmore journeyed to the Remington Works with the Sholes and Glidden machine which represented the culminating result of six years of inventive struggle. With him was George Washington Newton Yost, who had also become interested in the future possibilities of the "type-writer," and together they sought to persuade Philo Remington to take up the manufacture of the machine.

The story of the signing of the contract by which the Remingtons became the first makers of a commercially successful typewriter is told most interestingly by Henry Harper Benedict in the book recently published by the Herkimer County Historical Society and which was reviewed in the August issue of this magazine. It properly forms a part of this historical treatment and is reserved for later re-printing only because of the heavy demand made upon space in this special issue. Mr. Benedict was a clerk in the Remington establishment at the time and it was really through his influence that his employers were induced to father the undertaking. Here we wish to pay tribute to Mr. Benedict; he is the only man living who has gone through the entire 50 years here reviewed as a constant member of the industry, his present connection being that of a director of the Remington Typewriter Co.

The contract in creation of the Remington typewriter business was signed on March 1, 1873, and William K. Jenne was given the task of developing the machine for manufacturing and marketing. The next year he was made superintendent of the Typewriter Works, as separated from other departments, and for 30 years he continued in the same capacity; Mr. Jenne's name goes down as the dean of typewriter builders. Actual manufacture began in September, 1873, and the first Model 1 Remington was shipped from the factory early the next year. It wrote capital letters only and used the fundamental features of the inventor's model, worked into a machine that could be produced and sold in quantities. Many of these basic features, such as the escapement or letter spacing mechanism, the universal arrangement of the keyboard, hanging the typebars so that the type strike the paper at a common printing point and the carriage return

MODEL 1, No. 1, REMINGTON

mechanism still survive in typewriter construction. It resembled a sewing machine, with its stand and foot treadle for the return of the carriage, the Remingtons having been engaged in the manufacture of sewing machines on a large scale.

Densmore and Yost were the first selling agents, the Western Electric Company being given some territory. Then followed Densmore, Yost & Co., and after that the firm of Locke, Yost & Bates, composed of D. R. Locke, G. W. N. Yost and J. H. Bates. In July, 1878, Fairbanks & Company were made the selling agents, Clarence Walker Seamans being put in charge as manager of typewriter sales. And here begins the real story of the well directed effort to place the Remington typewriter in its proper light before the commercial world. For three years Mr. Seamans held his post with Fairbanks, E. Remington & Sons taking over the selling end of the business, in addition to manufacturing, in 1881. His former good work won for Seamans the appointment as sales head of their typewriter business. By this time, Remington Model 2 had been developed in solution of a very important problem, a machine which would write both capitals and small letters. This typewriter first appeared in 1878, and was the first machine which wrote both capitals and small letters, the product of several master minds in the Remington organization. William K. Jenne had a big hand in it. The problem of printing both capitals and small letters, with the standard keyboard arrangement, was solved by the combination of the cylinder shifting device, invented by Lucien S. Crandall, with type bars carrying two types, a capital and a small face of the same letter, invented by Bryon A. Brooks.

The ambition of Mr. Seamans led to the formation on August

1, 1882, of the famous firm of Wyckoff, Seamans & Benedict, who acquired the sales rights for the entire world. William Ozmun Wyckoff, Clarence Walker Seamans and Henry H. Benedict from their modest start at 281 Broadway, New York City, grew quickly out of their first quarters and moved to 334 Broadway in 1884. In March, 1886, they bought the typewriter business from E.

THE CAPITALS AND LOWER CASE MACHINE

Remington & Sons and it was removed from the gun factory to its own building in Ilion and W. K. Jenne installed as mechanical superintendent. In 1888, the New York general offices were moved to 327 Broadway, where they remained for almost 30 years. First, only the ground floor and basement was used, but in 1912 all of 19 floors in two buildings from 325 to 331 Broadway, comprising 58,000 sq. ft., were occupied.

In 1892, the co-partnership mentioned in the preceding paragraph was turned into a corporation embracing both manufacturing and selling activities and in 1903 the corporate name of Remington Typewriter Company with Mr. Benedict as its first president was adopted. Mr. Wyckoff died in 1895, Mr. Seamans in 1915, Mr. Benedict, as mentioned, being the surviving member of the original firm and the only living witness to the celebration of 50 years of Remington manufacture. "To save time is to lengthen life" was once a popularly used slogan in Remington marketing which comes to mind in review of the contribution to the extension of the world's business by those pioneers of the industry.

Remington Model No. 6 was first placed upon the market in the summer of 1894. The improvements, listed in a contemporaneous catalogue, were described as follows: "The adjustment of

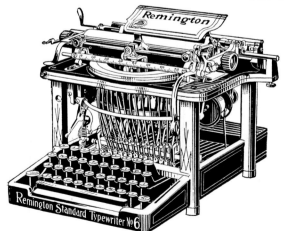

the cylinder, securing greater permanence for the original alignment of the machine; improved spacing mechanism; lighter and much improved paper carriage; improved ribbon movement; adjustable paper guides." This machine enjoyed wonderful popularity for more than fifteen years, and many of them are still in use. The Gorin tabulator was an addition in 1898, this being placed on the No. 7, which otherwise was practically the same as the now famous No. 6 Remington.

The Model 8 made its appearance in 1896. It was similar in appearance to the No. 6, but was especially designed for wide forms. Improved shifting mechanism and carriage support, an additional scale exhibiting position of carriage when raised, and a cylinder removable from the carriage were announced as new features. The standard size of this machine wrote a line 12 inches wide on paper of fourteen inches. Machines were also furnished that wrote a line sixteen inches long on paper 18 inches in width.

The Remington Vertical Accounting Machine was placed on the market in 1907. This was the first adding and subtracting typewriter. The Wahl adding mechanism was connected to the numeral keys of the then non-visible machine. The adding, furnished as a by-product of the writing, was, of course, a continued feature on the visible machine which came out the following year.

The Remington No. 10, placed upon the market in 1908, was the first visible typewriter sold by the Remington Company. It was designed to produce "More and Better Work." Later im-

provements of the No. 10 featured a new escapement, new type bar action, seven carriage improvements, improved ribbon mechanism and the "Natural Touch." It featured especially the "Self Starter," five keys used for automatically indenting the lines. This front stroke visible writing Remington was largely the work in its creation of Oscar Woodward.

An Improved Model 10 came out in July, 1915, October of the same year marking the election of Frank N. Kondolf as the successor to J. Walter Earle as president of the Remington Typewriter Co. Here can also be chronicled the regretable death of Mr. Earle on June 22, 1916. Likewise in an effort to include

events chiefly covering Remington history, the company moved from the long occupied premises at 325-331 to the present build-

ing housing the general offices at Broadway and White streets, New York City, on January 22, 1917.

Returning to the listing of models in the order of their appearance, the Remington No. 11 was first placed on the market in 1908. This machine is especially equipped for form and column figure work. It is provided with the built-in decimal tabulator, which gives ten different starting points in each column, and which permits the quick writing of units under units, tens under tens, etc.

The Remington 12, placed upon the market in 1922, embodies every Remington advantage, plus quiet action. Fourteen noise reducing features were introduced. The No. 12 has an improved

escapement, improved type bar construction, improved ribbon mechanism and refinements of construction throughout the entire machine. It also has the frame enclosed to keep out dust and dirt.

The Remington Accounting Machine was placed on the market in 1914. This machine contains every feature of the vertical adding machine, and in addition it adds across the page in the same operation. Any number of columns may be accumulated vertically, in addition to extending the cross total or balance. One of the common uses of this machine is for ledger posting where it is necessary to add the charge to or subtract the credit from the previous balance and extend the new balance, in addition to accumulating separate totals of debits and credits. This machine has been designed and is used for bookkeeping tasks of every kind.

Of course development work in all lines goes on continually, E. E. Barney, who was general manager of the Remington Works at Ilion, N. Y., from 1912 to 1918, being in general charge with headquarters in New York. One of the peculiarities of Mr. Barney's experience is that he has always been associated with the development and manufacture of front-stroke visible typewriters.

The Remington Portable, f i r s t placed upon the market in 1920, was the work of several Remington engineers. The governing ideas were a machine so light in weight that a child could carry it and so compact that it could be stored in any convenient place, and yet possessed of Remington durability a n d capacity for quality and quantity work. It has a unique method of

THE REMINGTON PORTABLE WITH ITS CARRYING CASE

raising the type to a printing position, and the standard four-bank keyboard. It also has other principal features of the office machines.

Remington history, as broadly heralded this year, covers 50 years, and it is difficult to embrace it all in a necessarily condensed treatment. The growth of the factory at Ilion; the first teaching of touch typewriting by Frank E. McGurrin, a clerk living in Grand Rapids, Mich., on the No. 1 Remington in 1878; the listing of Remington stocks on the New York Stock Exchange in August, 1919; the important elevation of men in the sales organization and the election of officers, including that of Benjamin L. Winchell to the Presidency in July, 1922; the placing of all manufacturing activities in the hands of F. W. Young as General Manager of Factories; all this and more could be elaborated upon in highly interesting narrative. The notable celebration at Ilion, New York, on September 12th is the subject of a special story appearing elsewhere in this issue.

Reliable

A single shift, 86 character machine of standard construction and size, designed to sell at a price below that of similar machines, is the Reliable typewriter appearing in 1921. It was invented by Arno Kührt and is manufactured by the Reliable Typewriter Co. G.m.b.H., of Nürnberg, Germany. The machine at its price is considered good value, it naturally making its strongest appeal from a price standpoint. In construction and general mechanism, it is noted that the Reliable bears a close similarity to the German made Commercial and Minerva machines. In some sections of Germany it is sold as the Belka typewriter by its representatives.

Reliance

The Reliance Typewriter Company was organized as a result of the purchase of assets of the defunct Pittsburgh Visible Typewriter Company related earlier in this compilation. The machine is an improvement over the last produced, the Pittsburgh Visible. The Reliance Company is located at Kittaning, Pa.

This machine has also been sold under various other names, including Wall Street, Broadway Standard, etc.

Remington-Sholes

Zalmon G. Sholes is recorded as the inventor of the Remington-Sholes, known in the industry as the Rem-Sho, though many like to believe that his father, C. Latham Sholes, was also responsible for features of this contribution to the writing machine industry. Presence of Remington in the name of the machine is accounted for by the partnership Sholes formed in 1893 with Franklin Remington, a son of one of the original Remingtons who started the manufacture of the Remington typewriter. Franklin Remington was general manager of the Remington-Sholes Company.

It was in 1896 when the Rem-Sho machines first began to come from the factory in Chicago. The keyboard was of standard four row arrangement with single shift, the keys being made of hard rubber. Although resembling the Remington, the machine had several interesting innovations of its own. Of this invisible writer, seven models were made. In 1908, a Remington-Sholes Visible was introduced as models 10 and 11, a standard four bank single shift machine of many good qualities that had been retained from its earlier form and adopted to visible writing.

THE VISIBLE TYPEWRITING
REMINGTON-SHOLES

Under the name of Remington - Sholes, later changed to Fay-Sholes as a result of litigation over use of the name "Remington," a new company was organized to acquire the Arithmograph, further reference to which will be found appropriately placed under the heading of Fay-Sholes for the purpose of identification. Another change in name was made to the Arithmograph Company when the

adding attachment was introduced as an integral part of the machine. Then followed liquidation of the latter named Arithmograph Company to make way for return to the first name, at

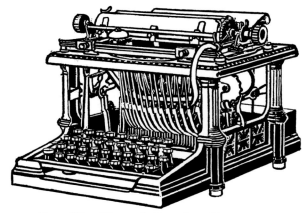

THE "NON-VISIBLE" REM-SHO TYPEWRITER
(ILLUSTRATION BY KINDNESS OF C. V. ODEN)

which time C. N. Fay was president of the company and the general offices and factory located at 127 Rees Street, Chicago.

Financial difficulties forced appointment of Chas. B. Price, secretary of the company, as Receiver on January 22, 1909. Later in the same year, he sold the machine with all tools and other equipment to Japy Freres & Company of Beaucourt, France, President Fay himself going overseas to supervise installation from which in due time a still further improved typewriter made its appearance in France as the Japy.

Rex

This was an entirely new creation by older interests in construction of typewriters, a full sized machine of standard qualification manufactured in a well equipped plant at Fond du Lac, Wisconsin.

With what was termed Model No. 4 of the Rex, the Rex Typewriter Company was announced as ready to do business in January, 1916, a company capitalized at $800,000 with B. E. Harris as president and H. M. Ballard as treasurer and general manager. The executive offices had been moved from the factory at Fond du Lac to 28 East Jackson Boulevard, Chicago. Rex No. 10, continuing the double shift with three banks of keys, came out in March, 1918. D. C. Harris was the inventor of all models of the Rex typewriter as well as its predecessor. Although now practically off the market, the Rex machine for several recent years was distributed in the United States and Canada by the Adding Machine Division of the American Can Co., which department the previously mentioned B. E. Harris managed after relinquishing his direct connection with the Rex company.

Rheinmetall

This machine appeared in 1921 as the product of the Rheinische Metallwaren & Maschinenfabrik of Düsseldorf, Germany, prominent German machinery manufacturers, who perfected their typewriter product as an adjunct to their line in the post-war period. The Rheinmetall is a typewriter of tested efficiency, single shift, 88 characters and all other necessary features of the modern writ-

ing machine. It has met with a popular demand since its inception. Sold in France by the agent there as the Metall, the Rheinmetall Handelsgesellschaft m.b.H., Berlin, W. 8, are the distributors in other markets under the name in the heading.

Roberts Ninety

Succeeding the Blick Ninety, so named to indicate its capacity of 90 characters, this machine was presented first in this trade paper in January, 1922. The L. R. Roberts Typewriter Company

also succeeded the Blick Typewriter Company, of Stamford, Conn., at the same time. The new incorporation was capitalized at $1,000,000 with C. Loomis Allen as president and George B. Brand as factory manager. L. R. Roberts, who died on December 21, 1921, was the inventor of the machine first bearing the Blick name and later that of his own.

Rochester

Inclusion in this historical treatment of a machine named the Rochester Portable, first presented in June of the current year by Rochester Industries, Incorporated, of Rochester, N. Y., recalls leading events in the forty years' practical engineering experience and typewriting machine designing by the inventor, Wellington P. Kidder.

Incorporating the Kidder Press Manufacturing Company in 1880, and for nearly fifteen years its chief engineer and treasurer, he designed a wide range of special adaptations of his self-feeding presses; used for printing the United States postal cards during the four years' contract of Woolworth and Graham; printing, consecutively numbering, perforating and slitting and rewinding a million two hundred and fifty thousand per day of the early strip tickets of the New York Elevated Railway; nearly 60 per cent of the countercheck slips used in the United States; millions of coupon railway tickets consecutively numbered and perforated; up to the Kidder twenty-two ton rotary web perfecting press for half tone engravings on which for many years the weekly editions of *The Buffalo Express* were printed.

Realizing the almost unlimited field of typewriting machines, his first typewriter invention was the Franklin in 1887—almost the pioneer in visible writing. This was followed by his Wellington

in 1892, claimed as the first visible typebar writing machine to insure permanent alignment, known in Canada, Belgium, Great Britain and colonies as the Empire and in Germany as the Adler, of which, it is estimated, there are now in everyday use over six hundred thousand.

Various features of his early inventions in these machines have been adopted and are now in use on nearly every typewriter on the market. Notably may be mentioned his guard enclosure of the ribbon spool, his priority of its invention duly sustained in the litigation that followed between leading typewriter companies. Also may be mentioned his Franklin typebar action now said by Mr. Kidder to be adopted on the new Remington Portable.

His pioneer conception of the well-known Noiseless typewriter, the only one to typewrite by silent leverage pressure as in a printing press, in place of the ordinary hammer blows, is con-

THE NEW ROCHESTER PORTABLE INVENTED BY WELLINGTON P. KIDDER

ceded. His design and construction of the first working models of this machine were made prior to 1896, on which he was granted a considerable number of United States patents and over twenty patents in other countries.

Now the consulting engineer of the Rochester Industries, Incorporated, and inventor and designer of the Rochester Portable and the Rochester Silent typewriters, it is the good fortune of Mr. Kidder to present what he terms the most valuable and crowning achievements of his career.

Notwithstanding so many excellent writing machines of various makes in use, there is ample room for these further contributions. The Rochester Portable is a visible writer of hardened steel, simple and durable, less than six pounds in weight, half the size of the average portable typewriter, a good manifolder, with perfect alignment, writing 84 characters with speed and excellence. Morton H. Anderson is president of the enterprise organized to market the latest inventions of that pioneering typewriter man, Wellington P. Kidder.

Rofa

A development of the Faktotum machine appearing on the market in 1921 and manufactured by Robert Fabig G.m.b.H., of Neurippen, Germany, and distributed by the Rofa Schreibmaschinen G.m.b.H., of Berlin, is the Rofa 30-key, double-shift machine with a greatly improved inking system. It has an ingenious application of the ink roll principle and provides usual features demanded today in the more moderate priced machines.

Royal

The technical history of the Royal typewriter is a narrative from its inception to the present day of the original and subsequent inventions of E. B. Hess, vice-president, a director and member of the executive committee of the Royal Typewriter Company, a rather unique and advantageous position which is not usually accorded an inventor of a product. But ever since the entry into the industry of the Royal Typewriter Company in 1906 as a vehicle for exploitation of his inventions, Mr. Hess has been steadfast in his active prominence and untiring in his work of mechanical development.

The efforts of Mr. Hess have always been devoted to processes having to do with visible writing machines. His first patents related to a nine bar typewriter, carrying upon its free end a revolving sleeve having nine printing characters thereon and making a printing capacity of 81 characters. Upon completion, Mr. Hess himself declared it a "freak" type of machine and not commercially acceptable. It was, however, the incentive to interest him in the higher development or refinement of the art as then known.

Having in mind certain insufficiencies in the behavior of keyboard actions, he deemed it necessary to make a radical departure and the result was an innovation in the typewriter art. This conception is known as a reverse or accelerating toggle typebar movement which affords a light initial touch to the finger key and imparts to the typebar rapidly increasing speed as it makes its excursion to the printing point. This, like all of the inventions of Mr. Hess relating to the typewriter art made since 1902, numbering over 140 patents, are the property of the Royal Typewriter Company, Inc., whose general offices are at 364 Broadway, New York City, and manufacturing plant at Hartford, Conn.

In further relation of mechanical conceptions, the anti-friction roller escapement which is the connecting link between the keyboard and the carriage was perfected by Mr. Hess. This combination of the accelerating typebar and anti-friction roller escapement yielded a clear, decisive and refined printing result which gave birth to the Royal advertising slogan—"Compare the work." Following this serious consideration was expended upon the form that the carriage should take with respect to eliminating or overcoming, to the greatest extent, the factor of friction when moving step by step. The mono-rail idea appealed as the solution; i. e., a single track containing a pair of bearing balls surrounded by individual pinions, coacting with a stationary and movable rack. This brought the creation of a new mechanical principle.

It was found that such relation of parts could be advantageously used in conjunction with the further idea of elevating all carriage parts simultaneously from normal to shifting position, including the roller escapement mechanism, and from this unusual combination of elements it has been possible to lock the carriage definitely and positively in either the normal or shifted positions and, also, in any position of its travel; thereby was made a great contribution to maintenance of alignment.

The paper feed, which had always been considered a "bane" of the typewriter's performance, was solved by an unusual combination of levers and locations of the feed rolls and were so combined by Mr. Hess with the pressure devices at and above the printing point that any kind of card, envelope or writing material, single or in usable quantities, can be successfully fed and printed upon any area thereof by mechanisms which are inbuilt in the Royal structure and therefore requiring no added attachments for the purpose.

There are about twenty exclusive Hess patented features in the Royal typewriter which do not appear in any other product. One among them is the combination stop block for limiting the right and left margins and also for tabular work and line locking, all accomplished through a single swinging element. In those mentioned and all others, there are no accidents in the contributions of Mr. Hess to the typewriter art, each of the features being the result of concentration and application to achieve a result hitherto not attained and with maximum simplicity, durability, ease of operation, and a clear and definite printing result in mind. His last serious effort of accomplishment and recorded embodiment into the product of his company was in the nature of adopting the accelerating typebar movement to affect a noise reduction from the typebar impact with the platen. This is illustrated mechanically in the latest "Q" or Quiet model of the Royal No. 10. The essence of this invention resides in bringing the typebar, by the actuation of the finger key, to what is known as the "momentum period," which is about fifteen degrees from the printing point.

In addition to noise reduction Mr. Hess accomplished what is claimed to be a new attainment in the typewriter art. As the typebar moves through the momentum period, its then relation to the step by step movement of the carriage makes it impossible for this machine to skip, pile or overprint, or to make double impressions, familiarly known as "feathering." Of this latter achievement Mr. Hess is justly particularly proud. Throughout his inventive activity, the vision of the typist was constantly before him, realizing that not only visibility in its most highly developed form was important but also that availability was a

desideratum; i. e., to excel in accessibility to insert material to be fed, making insertions, correction of errors, changing of ribbons, etc.

Truly, the world-wide selling organization of the Royal Typewriter Company has been well cared for in the furnishing of a product. From the first shop of 744 sq. ft., the Brooklyn fac-

THE PRESENT DAY ROYAL TYPEWRITER

tory at 45th Street and Second Avenue, the breaking of ground on May 4, 1911, for the new Hartford factory on up through the addition of wings to its present floor space of 350,000 sq. ft. for the exclusive manufacture of Royal typewriters this enterprise has grown with the mechanical and marketing organizations in close harmony. From general sales manager to the presidency on January 1, 1914, George Ed Smith has been a notable figure in Royal history; he is the executive head of 123 branch offices in principal cities of the U. S. and distributing agencies in every country of the world under the direction of T. T. Malleson. It would make a long list were attempt made to mention all who have been and are prominently identified with the Royal undertaking; no small amount of romance is attached to remembrance of the days when Philip T. Dodge, Grant Hugh Browne and Joseph M. Stoughton officered the company, respectively as president, treasurer and secretary, together with the plural introduction in 1906 of the Royal Standard and the Royal Grand, the later improvement of the former low-framed machine and its advent as the No. 5, etc., but brevity is the governing factor in this compilation and we are obliged to turn to the next subject in alphabetical order.

Salter

Although there is in course of preparation an entirely different machine which will be known under another name and for the marketing of which a contract has been entered into with London

interests headed by George G. Rimington, the Salter typewriter known well to sellers and users since 1892 requires mention in this history.

The famous old firm of George Salter & Company in West Bromwich, England, were the earliest to enter the field among the many English typewriter manufacturing efforts of which few survived. The Salter typewriter was invented by James S. Foley of London and brought out at a much lower price than the competing American machines on the British market at the time. It was of typebar construction with the bars erect like in the original Bar-Lock when in normal position, but utilizing an ink pad instead of a ribbon for writing. Very shortly after its introduction, however, ribbon mechanism was applied to all Salter machines.

The earlier models contained three rows of keys with double

shift, but the later machines had four banks of 42 keys with one shift key. A good many different models were made, terminating in the last visible, single shift machine which came out in 1907. The English workmanship as exemplified in the Salter typewriter has always been excellent and wherever the machines were used have given ample satisfaction. This writing machine product has also been sold under the names of Perfect and Royal Express.

Saturn

Neither a typebar, type wheel or indicator machine, but something entirely different was the Saturn of 1897. Shifting was made unnecessary by the construction of this machine, it utilizing a printed chart for a keyboard, arranged by rows and with nine keys for printing purposes. This was an entirely new thought in writing machine construction, which, however, did not succeed. The Saturn was produced by E. Stauder of Zurich and invented by F. Meyer-Teuber, also of Switzerland.

Saxonia

Distributed by Messrs. Franz Lippmann, Saxonia Schreibmaschinen, Mülheim, Ruhr, Germany, this product is a standard four-row single shift machine of the usually accepted modern construction, containing first class materials and having all the necessary features. It is sold at a very moderate price and is creating a place for itself on the market.

Schade

A machine very similar to Pastor Hansen's early writing machine with keyboard arranged spherically was the Schade of 1896. It had combination keys and bars of practically one piece which struck downward onto the paper carriage beneath. Rudolf Schade of Berlin was the inventor; he was a German university professor.

Schapiro

Another indicator type of machine employing a type wheel for writing was the Schapiro of 1894. It was similar to the Crown which is of later date. The right hand was used to move the indicator to the desired letter and the left to depress the single writing key which brought the type wheel into contact with the platen, descriptive language which is almost identical to that for many other writing devices embraced by this story. A. Schapiro, of Berlin, the German duplicator man of fame through his invention of the Schaporigraph, was the inventor of the typewriter recorded by this paragraph, but he soon abandoned his typewriter effort to devote all of his activity to the duplicator business.

Schiesari

The Syllable Typewriter Company, 16-18 Exchange Place, New York City, was organized in 1914 for the purpose of manufacturing the Schiesari syllable and word writing typewriter originated in Turin, Italy, but the project was not carried to a point of introduction of the product.

Schinowara

A government official in the Banking Bureau of the Department of Finance of Japan, M. Schinowara, was credited in February, 1908, with invention of a machine for the Chinese and Japanese which would write ideographs. It was said to be about one foot square and capable of writing 2,500 signs or signals per minute, a more or less unlikely claim.

Secor

Jerome B. Secor, inventor of the Secor, spent ten years from 1901 upon perfecting his typewriter. He laid great stress upon solving of the alignment question and his machine, which came out in 1911, had much to recommend it. Four banks of keys, single shift and front stroke typebar action were features in a machine which seemed destined for greater things, were it not for its superfluity of parts and consequent impracticability as an economic manufacturing proposition. The Secor contained most of the modern demands in typewriter construction, together with features of its own such as an escapement which could readily be removed from the machine. It had a distinctive typebar action and an effective tabulator peculiarly its own.

The Secor was manufactured by the Secor Typewriter Company at Derby, Conn., in the old Williams factory. The Secor company was the successor to the Williams Typewriter Company. About 7,000 Secor typewriters were made up to the time of its

regretable disappearance from the field. In January, 1916, the plant in which the Secor typewriter had been manufactured was sold to the Maxim Munitions Corporation for the making of cartridges.

Senator

One of Germany's very recent presentations of the standard variety, the Senator, is a front stroke, segment, typebar, single shift, 90 character typewriter with many other useful features that promise for it a successful future. The machine appeared first in 1922. It has a removable basket for multi-language purpose and a lifting carriage for easy cleaning. The Senator is manufactured by the Falcon Werke A-G., at Darmstadt, Germany.

Senta

The portable typewriter product to which much of the effort of the manufacturers, Frister & Rossmann Aktiengesellschaft, of Berlin, is devoted. It first appeared in 1912, selling in Ger-

many at the equivalent of $50. Formerly, the enterprise emanating from the original partnership of Messrs. Frister & Rossmann made the larger machine referred to elsewhere under their firm name, the fabrication of the Senta succeeding the earlier Frister & Rossmann typewriter. In the portable class, but forming a happy and clever combination between the heavier office machines and the light weight traveling typewriters, the Senta is taxing the capacity of the makers to fill the demand. One of the best of German made typewriters is the present product.

Prior to adoption of its present name, the Senta typewriter appeared in less improved form as the product of Frister & Rossmann of Berlin and was sold for some time starting in 1903 as the Presto by Ulrich Nordmann of Dresden, Germany.

Shilling

Distributed for a short period beginning late in 1921 by the Shilling Brothers Typewriter Company, 428 Fourth Ave., Pittsburgh, Pa., a well-known dealership of that city, the typewriter they handled was called the Shilling Brothers. With the exception of the name, the machine was the same as the Reliance typewriter manufactured by the Reliance Machine Mfg. Co. of Kittaning, Pa. The project was abandoned a few months back.

Shimer

This machine showed every evidence during years from 1898 on of momentary appearance on the market, but the manufacturers announced from time to time that it was withheld from the market and it finally was forgotten as a possibility, though there are many men in the business even today who will recall the Shimer typewriter.

Sholes Visible

In 1909 a typewriter of peculiar construction and named as above was brought out by the C. Latham Sholes Typewriter Manufacturing Company of Milwaukee, Wis. Louis Sholes, an  elder son of the original inventor of the first practical writing machine, was the inventor of the latest Sholes Visible and vice-president of the company named after his illustrious parent. Louis Sholes was a practical printer, had been connected closely with writing machine inventing since youth and took the first paging machine of his father to Chicago for demonstration.

As indicated above, the Sholes Visible typewriter was different from others to the extent of being an oddity. The typebars when at rest reposed in projection at the front of the machine, which can be seen in the accompanying illustration. Upon striking a key, the typebar left its normal position, moved out into a sort of runway between the two rows of bars and travelled with frontstroke motion to the printing point on the platen. The result was visible, but, while ingenious, the action of the typebars had a tendency to retard, rather than enhance, speed. It had the standard keyboard of today, which, by the way, was adopted by C. Latham Sholes through the suggestion of this son, Louis Sholes, who not only helped his father greatly in other directions, but gave much thought to rearrangement of the "printers' case" to something more convenient to both hands.

An earlier appearance of practically the same machine was in 1901, said to be the last participation in inventive effort by C. Latham Sholes. It was put out by the Meiselbach Typewriter Company of Kenosha, Wisconsin, and was also named the Sholes Visible. Some have listed this typewriter as the Meiselbach.

Silent

This name was much in the minds and conversation of typewriter men 25 years ago as a coming machine of which much was expected. A noiseless typewriter it was, the bringing to life by slow inventive stages of a machine which is today much in evidence as a factor. Pressure of the type against the paper, instead of blows, by the use of a joint behind each typebar was the original method in operation when it was called the Silent. Now the industry has the Noiseless typewriter, which was the outcome of the machine here listed.

Simplex

For a brief period before the war the No. 10 Smith Premier typewriter was offered in Germany as the Simplex typewriter, the latter without decimal tabulator, stencil cutter, two-color ribbon and similar features but taking nothing away from its sturdiness or writing ability. This was done only to make it possible to sell the machine at a considerably reduced price and thus cater to that clientele demanding a lower priced machine. Supply of Simplex machines ceased with the war.

Harry A. Smith

The undertaking headed by the gentleman whose name as per above was incorporated into title of company and machine seems almost to have been doomed from the start. There has been more said about it since its troubles began than before. A suc-

cession of misfortunes they were, for the Harry A. Smith typewriter had merit and its sponsor highly deserved the place in the manufacturing branch of the industry which his ambitions prompted.

The product was the former Blick Bar. Although there was an earlier company, reorganization in December, 1920, brought into being the Harry A. Smith Typewriter Company with capital

stock of $800,000. This relates to formation of an organization at Elkhart, Indiana, a move from Chicago having taken place about a year before. But plans did not work out and in February, 1921, a receiver was appointed in the person of W. E. Wider. A local party bought in the ground and factory buildings, but effort is still continued to dispose of the patents and manufacturing tools.

L. C. Smith

The connection of Wilbert L. Smith, now president of the L. C. Smith & Bros. Typewriter Company, with the typewriter industry covers a period of 38 years. In the fall of 1885 he became associated with A. T. Brown, also of Syracuse, N. Y., in the development of a typewriting machine, and in the fall of 1888 a partnership by this Mr. Smith with his older brother, Lyman C. Smith, was formed, operating under the name of the Smith Premier Typewriter Company. Lyman C. Smith was manufacturing guns in Syracuse, N. Y. With him in the gun business were associated the one mentioned together with two other brothers, Monroe C. Smith and Hurlbut W. Smith. In 1888 the first model of the Smith Premier typewriter was made and in 1890 it was put on the market and met with success.

The Smith brothers soon placed the Smith Premier Company in a prominent position, so that on March 1, 1893, when the Union Typewriter Company of America was formed, the Smith Premier

MODEL 8, THE LATEST L. C. SMITH & BROS. TYPEWRITER

Company became one of the units of that organization, along with the Remington, Yost, Caligraph and Densmore. Lyman C. Smith was also the first vice-president of the Union amalgamation until 1896, when he resigned and W. L. Smith was elected in his place.

For ten years Lyman C. Smith continued as president of the Smith Premier Typewriter Company, Wilbert L. Smith as vice-president and factory manager, Monroe C. Smith as secretary and

Hurlbut W. Smith as treasurer. On January 27, 1903, announcement was made of the resignation of all four of the Smiths from the Union Typewriter Company and of the organization of the L. C. Smith & Bros. Typewriter Co. to manufacture a visible writing machine. A site was purchased in East Washington Street and work was immediately started on an eight-story factory. This was added to in 1909 by the building of the north wing, which practically doubled the capacity of the original building.

While the work of construction was going on the Smith Brothers rented a suite of offices in the Nottingham Building, Syracuse. December 10, 1903, they occupied for the first time

THE L. C. SMITH & BROS. TYPEWRITER, MODEL 2

offices in the new factory in East Washington Street. The typewriter which the Smiths were to market was the invention of Carl Gabrielson, who is still with the company.

The first machine made was Model 2 and was shipped out from the factory November 26, 1904. The first Model 1 machine was shipped out February 2, 1905. Model 1 differed from Model 2 only in having 76 instead of 84 characters.

At that time a battle was raging in the typewriter world between those who believed in the "writing in sight" principle and those who favored the old "blind" idea. The Smith Brothers had a number of signs made for the outside of their building, which adjoins the New York Central railroad tracks. Some of these signs read as follows: "You are Right Side Up; Why Write Upside Down?" "When Precedent and Progress clash, we forsake Precedent." "Writing in Sight is in Line with Progress." There were eighteen of these signs altogether and they made a great impression upon the passengers of the New York Central who saw them. When the Smith Brothers threw their hat into

the ring for the visible principle, it seemed to settle the discussion and now all manufacturers of typewriters recognize the principle of visibility.

The L. C. Smith typewriter from the start had several exclusive features, which have later been added to. Probably the most revolutionary of these was the

MODEL 5 WAS PLACED ON THE MARKET IN NOVEMBER, 1911

shifting of the type segment instead of shifting the carriage, and the interchangeable platen feature. The ball bearing feature has also been one of the mechanical principles which has made the L. C. Smith typewriter a success. The machine is ball bearing throughout, in the typebar joints, the carriage runways and the shifting mechanism. From time to time improvements have been added, resulting in the Model 5, the first of which was shipped November 1, 1911, and the latest—Model 8—with right or left carriage return, which was brought out about the first of August, 1915. The following features of Model 8 are described in the catalog: Silence of operation, variable line spacing platen, light touch, standard keyboard, flexible paper feed, paper fingers, protected type, key controlled ribbon, lightning escapement, line space regulator, ribbon guard, line lock, back space, margin release, paper release, bill and paper guide, period and comma stops.

In addition to a number of improvements over Model 5, the No. 8 is silent running.

The L. C. Smith typewriter is sold through branches, sub-branches and dealers in every city in the United States and in almost every foreign country, including China, Japan, India, the Philippines, Dutch East Indies, Australia, South Africa, British East Africa, France and her African colonies, Austria, Belgium, Denmark, Finland, Germany, Greece, Holland, Italy, Jugo-Slavia, Czecho-Slovakia, Latvia, Lithuania, Norway, Poland, Portugal, Russia, Spain, Sweden, Switzerland, Great Britain, Argentina, Bolivia, Brazil, Chile, Colombia, Ecuador, Peru, Paraguay, Uruguay, Venezuela, Honduras, Costa Rica, Guatemala, Nicaragua, Panama, Salvador, Cuba, Dominican Republic, Haiti, Mexico, Hawaii, Azores, Canaries and many others.

Lyman C. Smith, president of the company, died November 5, 1910, and Monroe C. Smith died July 24, 1914.

The present officers of the company are: Wilbert L. Smith, president, and Hurlbut W. Smith, secretary and treasurer, the two surviving of the original four Smith brothers.

Smith Premier

In 1889, the Smith Premier typewriter first came into being, the invention of Alexander T. Brown. As is generally known in the business, it was originally a so-called blind writer and was

THE NON-VISIBLE MACHINE, No. 2 MODEL

always a double keyboard machine up until the time of the advent of an entirely new product. This new machine was announced last month.

The No 2 Smith Premier was the most popular of the non-visible models, its easy action and light touch filling the bill completely in its intended succession to the Caligraph. Like the last named, it was one of the machines embraced by the amalgamation under the parent company, the Union Typewriter Company.

The phrase "a key for every character" belongs purely to the Smith Premier, although used by others and by ourselves more

than once in this narrative by way of description of other makes. That feature was retained even when visible writing was adopted with advent of the No. 10 in November, 1908, one month after the Remington Visible came out. In 1909 E. E. Bar-

THE VISIBLE SMITH PREMIER TYPEWRITER OF 1908

ney was placed at the head of the manufacturing activities of the newly introduced visible writing Smith Premier, he being superintendent and general manager of the factory at Syracuse, N. Y., from the year mentioned until 1912.

As announced in the April, 1923, issue of this trade paper, the Smith Premier Typewriter Company was then re-organized with George W. Dickerman as president and Wm. T. Humes as vice-president, the new single shift Smith Premier being the vehicle for creation and maintenance of a manufacturing and marketing organization distinctly its own. The new machine was first shown to the trade in the last number of this trade paper as the Smith Premier 60. It is the invention of Jacob Felbel. Among the emphasized features of the new shift key Smith Premier are open face construction, extra size platen cylinder, four posi-

THE NEW SHIFT KEY SMITH PREMIER TYPEWRITER

tion ribbon adjustment, typebar segment shift, 46 keys with printing capacity of 92 characters and a cushion like touch.

Soblik

This was a pneumatic typewriter invented by a man of the same manner, an engineer of Düsseldorf, Germany. Only hand-made models of the Soblik were constructed. It weighed 7 kilograms (15½ pounds) and its dimensions were 30x25x15 centimeters (12x10x6 inches). It was visible writing and practically noiseless.

Sphinx

A single-shift, 84-character typewriter was the Sphinx, representing a further effort to establish Switzerland as a producer of writing machines. It was a standard machine in every detail except perhaps in its typebar mechanism, which resembled greatly that of the Franklin. Effort was originally expended upon the Sphinx in 1913 but it was abandoned at the outbreak of the war. It was manufactured by the S. A. Sphinx, Fleurier, Switzerland, and was the invention of S. Gertsch.

Stallman

A small machine weighing only 2½ pounds invented by F. G. Stallman, 45 West 126th Street, New York City, the Stallman was made known to the industry only in April of the current year. It utilizes a type wheel.

Standard Folding

For lack of better reason, the large number of typewriters whose names begin, or began, with the letter "s" gives an excuse for placing the Standard Folding in this classification as a proposition

justifying mention of its own. At that, this little machine which broke the ice in many respects in the portable field and was first to offer the advantage of being folded up into small space, had some history which antedated the time when the Standard Typewriter Company took it over and later renamed it Corona.

We may be pardoned for saying that it was first described in this trade paper in September, 1907. In those days it had a long name, being called "The Standard Folding Type-Bar Visible Writing Typewriter." But, even though long in title, it was short in weight in fulfillment of its claim to being portable, weighing 5½ lbs. in its first model. The first machines were sold in 1907, the factory and general offices being located in New York City; the office of the president of the original company, M. W. Hazen, was at 27 Thames st. and the manufacturing plant was on West 26th street, the latter being in charge of George F. Rose, still a figure of prominence in inventive capacity living for the most part on his farm at Hyndsville, New York.

In 1902, Frank S. Rose, father of the Mr. Rose mentioned in the preceding paragraph, conceived the idea of producing a practical typebar portable typewriter to meet his vision of an age when mechanical writing would be universal and not alone confined to business correspondence. His study of the requirements of such a machine called for flexibility, compactness, light weight and a radical departure from the then existing types of machines. As part of his problem was the reduction of weight, he determined upon the use of formed sheet metal for frame construction, and this new feature of typewriter engineering has played a bigger part in the success of this class of writer than is generally recognized.

Development work was carried on from 1902 to 1905, when the elder Mr. Rose died. It then became necessary for the son, George F. Rose, to continue his work and secure finances for establishment of a manufacturing plant. The father would probably have contributed still further to the art had he lived to see his first practical typebar portable typewriter such a successful article of economic value as it exists today in Corona, but the mantle in falling upon the shoulders of the son suffered no discontinuance in activity in carrying out of plans and the Rose Typewriter Company was formed. Instant demand after start to make the Standard Folding in 1907 proved the correctness of the inventor's vision and profited those who financed it.

The illness and death in 1909 of M. W. Hazen, who had supplied the money until then to carry on the work, caused George F. Rose to seek a re-financing of the company and Senator Benn Conger became interested. One of the first whom he brought into the undertaking was Carlton F. Brown, whom the historian of this compilation vividly recalls as the chief buffer for the grief encountered. The Standard Typewriter Company was formed, as told in the separate Corona story, and the resourceful Brown dealt successfully with all obstacles, including one J. A. Whitcomb et. al., who, as the former sales agents in marketing the product as the Standard Folding Sales Co., continued to sell machines covered by the patents which Mr. Brown and his associates had legally acquired. The fight was started because the new owners declined to take over with the Rose Typewriter Company a voided contract with the Sales Company; Whitcomb, it was alleged, began to manufacture an infringement, but he was eventually stopped by a permanent injunction.

Stearns

E. C. Stearns & Co., Syracuse, N. Y., makers of other metal products which equipped them to undertake a typewriter venture, added the invention of J. E. Thomas, now head of the

Typewriter Inspection Company in New York, as well as features invented by August Schneelock, and launched into the making of the Stearns Visible typewriter in November, 1905. Machines were pronounced ready and offered to the buying public late in 1908, a product of the standard variety which embraced all modern requirements of the day and a number of anticipatory features.

The Stearns typewriter was a front stroke, typebar, entirely visible, universal keyboard of four rows, single shift and 84 character machine. It had a unique typebar action and contained not a few features of merit which as recalled create a feeling of regret that it could not have been continued. Manufacture was discontinued several years ago.

An event which attracted no little attention in connection with plans for marketing of the Stearns was the acquisition as a member of the organization in December, 1909, of George M. Moore of London. Mr. Moore had for 18 years been general manager for the Williams Typewriter Company in Europe and transferred his affiliation to take up general direction of Stearns sales in all of Europe from an office located in London.

Through its representative in Germany, Guhl & Harbeck, the Stearns typewriter for a short time starting in 1908 was sold in that country as the Guhl.

Sterling

The Sterling Typewriter Company, 115 Broadway, New York City, started business in January, 1911. The product was called  the Sterling and was invented by C. J. Paulson. The selling price at retail was placed at $25. H. M. Nelson, with an office at 143 Liberty St., New York City, had the foreign selling rights in his hands and in April of the year that the Sterling was put on the market a branch office was opened at 38 to 40, Lloyd St., Albert Square, Manchester, England, for the handling of British business; the latter was in charge of Edward C. Pepper.

Sterling Fox

The suffix of Fox which we use in the heading to distinguish this machine from the one referred to in the immediately preceding paragraph was not used with all offerings of it, this product

from the factory of the Fox Typewriter Company at Grand Rapids, Michigan, more often being known by the title of Sterling alone. It was a portable, double shift machine unlike the Baby Fox, weighing 7½ pounds and of sturdy construction. It disappeared with the general unfortunate breaking up of Fox typewriter production.

Stoewer

In a factory established in 1857 and manufacturing sewing machines and bicycles, Bernh. Stoewer, of Stettin, Grunhof, Germany, have been making  the Stoewer typewriters of standard 90 character model since 1903. Carl Wasmuth, now deceased, was the leading spirit in the Stoewer typewriter undertaking and he gave to it an impetus during his life that has thoroughly established the name Stoewer as one to be reckoned with in typewriter manufacture. A new model in April, 1909, was called the Stoewer Record, the same machine selling in the British market as the Swift at a price of £22:0:0 to £23:10:0. A portable machine,

called the Stoewer Elite and likewise illustrated herewith, was added to the line in December, 1912.

Since the inauguration of this writing machine enterprise, officially titled Nähmaschinen- und Fahrräder-Fabrik Bernh. Stoewer, Actiengesellschaft, five models of standard typewriters  have been made, named the Stoewer I, II, III, IV and the latest, the Stoewer Record. A Stoewer Record foolscap, a 14¾" and an 18¾" carriage machine are also supplied, for which the manufacturer supplied illustrating cliches for use in this story but which, like in many other instances, we are unable to show because of heavy demand upon space. More than brief mention of the works at Stettin, where a working staff of 2,500 people is employed, is also prevented, but it can be said that the plant equipment is constantly being added to through an ever increasing demand for the Stoewer products. One of the most prominent machines on the continent, several awards of prizes which include seven gold medals for high class workmanship indicate the merit of the Stoewer typewriter.

Late printed matter issued by the manufacturers in presentation of the Stoewer Record mentions government, municipal and business offices as big users and 27 machines sold to the Bulgarian government is noted. Features enumerated include visible writing, writing speed from 11 to 14 letters per second; 44 keys in four banks and single shift, 90 characters to the line, easy and noiseless carriage movement and absolute guarantee of materials and workmanship. The Stoewer Elite, the portable machine, sells at £12:10:0 without and £12:15:0 with a carrying case and offers visibility, removable typebars, bichrome ribbon, writing on ruled paper, reliable escapement, compactness, double shift with 90 characters, ball bearing carriage, left and right marginal release, etc. The Stoewer Elite machine was for a while sold in France as the Dactylotypea Stoewer.

Sun

The Sun Typewriter Company was created in 1885 by the late Lee S. Burridge, who inaugurated the policy of strict adherence to the production of moderate priced typewriting machines to which the company has consistently held.

Its first production was a stylus operated machine of which many thousands were sold, resulting in a very prosperous business for a decade and a half. During this period, there was constructed and tested 685 models of typewriters in the effort to produce a thoroughly efficient typebar machine which could be profitably sold commercially.

This experimental and development work resulted in placing on the market in 1901 the first front strike visible writing typebar machine sold at a so-called popular or moderate price. A fairly profitable sale of this machine at a retail price of $40 with regular iron and steel frame and $45 in aluminum indicated the commercial possibilities of the model, which was quickly improved and marketed as Sun No. 2. This model has had an uninterrupted sale since its introduction and its continued manufacture is anticipated. The characteristic element in the Model No. 2 was the employment of the direct inking principle which not only produces exquisite work but is claimed to permit more and better carbon copies than when the conventional inked ribbon is employed.

This feature soon brought many requests for a more pretentious machine, resulting in the production of the Sun Model

No. 3 priced at $75, which was designed specifically for commercial usage. Following this, several others, including the No. 6, have been produced until a total of nine models have been created and marketed. Among these models is the Sun Check Writer which has the unique feature of protecting the checks with no further detail or labor than the writing of them, the direct inking feature permitting the perforation of the check and printing the face of the type on the face of the check. The present production comprises the No. 2, Mercantile Model, Special Sun Model and the Sun Check Writer.

In 1906 the company brought out the Aluminum travellers model, one of the early portable typebar machines placed on the market. Its weight is 10 pounds and many thousands have been sold.

The representative in Germany in 1913, Carl E. Lehmann, Frankfurt a.M., sold the Sun typewriter as the Carlem, a larger machine than the Leframa which he similarly sold.

Since the death of Lee S. Burridge on May 4, 1915, the company has been headed by his brother, F. O. Burridge. The personnel of the company is of long standing, Chas. W. Howell at present rounding out his 25th year of connection. The policy is unchanged with the exception that a specialty has been made of foreign markets for their products.

In the research work continuously carried out by the company many valuable inventions applying to typewriters have been perfected, causing an over-flow. which has resulted in these in-

ventions being adopted by other companies and included in many commercial typewriter successes. It is safe to say that there is no mechanical principle extant that has not been very carefully analyzed and experimented with as to their application to typewriter mechanism and particularly with reference to the production of moderate priced machines.

Lee S. Burridge was always an ardent investigator of mechanical means and he had perhaps the most diversified knowledge of typewriter patents of anyone in the art. His interest in the production of typewriters was created years before he finally entered into the business and his deductions and policies have become fixed principles with the Sun company in the production of its typewriting machines.

Stolzenberg

The Oliver typewriter when originally introduced into Germany was known as the Stolzenberg, that machine having been represented and assembled in Germany, from parts shipped in bulk from America, by Fabrik Stolzenberg of Oos-Baden. The same concern now distribute as their own a typewriter recently announced as the Stolzenberg-Fortuna.

The Oliver Model V was sold in Germany in 1907 by Fabrik Stolzenberg G.m.b.H., of Oos Baden, under the name of the "Fiver."

Swift

The model of the Stoewer typewriter which was introduced in 1909 and made by Bernh. Stoewer at Stettin, Grunhof, Germany, was placed on the British Isles market under the name of the Swift. It was identical with the Stoewer Record except in name.

Taylor

An electric typewriter was evolved in 1910 by Joseph Taylor, of Rochester, N. Y., which was named after the inventor in the effort that was made to find a manufacturer for it. The Taylor was frequently referred to at the time as the most practical electrically driven writing machine ever worked out. It was abandoned in November, 1910, only a few months after it first appeared.

Teletype

A machine for typewriting and at the same time transmitting by wire the same matter to another and which employed the Hammond as its typewriting mechanism is worthy of mention; it was called the Teletype.

Telewriter

The fore part of the paragraph about the Teletype applies to another so-called "distance writer" called the Telewriter and first mentioned briefly in October, 1907.

Tell

This portable typewriter, formerly called the Mitex, is manufactured by the Tell Schreibmaschinen G.m.b.H., Spandau-West, Germany. The machine appeared originally in 1922 and presents several innovations in typewriter construction. The Tell weighs about 8 lbs. and is of double shift. It is manufactured under the unit system, having, it is claimed, only 170 different parts and is an exceptionally fast assembling job. Its bars are all of equal length, permitting an even touch and uniformity in impression, and the carriage can be raised for ready cleaning of the inward mechanism. Instead of the usual cast or aluminum frame, the Tell housing is composed of thin steel upon the exterior of which is applied a fibre of long wearing quality similar to the fibrous "Sanitas" made in America. This adds greatly to the beauty of the machine with out sacrificing durability.

Tilden-Jackson

Hamilton, Ont., was the location of the Tilden-Jackson Typewriter Company organized with $500,000 of capital stock and with a factory built to manufacture a typewriter. Its affairs were wound up in 1908.

Titania

The Titania Typewriter Company, G.m.b.H., of Berlin, Germany, was formed in September, 1910. The Titania machine, which was a standard front stroke, single shift product, was first made in the manufacturing plant of Mix & Genest, of the same city. John Birney, for many years with the Remington, was general manager in marketing of the Titania, said to be the first ball-bearing type bar machine made in Germany.

Model 3 was offered in 1913. Mr. Birney resigned as a director in January, 1922, and has given his chief attention since to other work. The present Titania company is a subsidiary of the famous German Telephone Company, G.m.b.H., of Berlin. As to the present Titania product, it is a thoroughly modern typewriter, with a shifting type basket, rather than carriage, adopting it well to wide carriage work.

Torpedo

This machine was first heard of in March, 1907, so far as our records go, though another authority says that Torpedo typewriters have been made since 1893. In any event, this writing

machine product was placed on the market by Gebr. Weil, of Frankfurt-Rödelheim, Germany. In 1908 the business was incorporated under the title of Weil-Werke Ges. m. b. H., with capital of 1,200,000 marks. The Torpedo is a front stroke, four bank machine of standard make, the No. 5 model introduced in 1911 being the last to appear except for periodical refinements which have kept it up-to-date.

The typewriter appearing first in 1907 as the Torpedo is the same in improved form as the Hassia machine introduced in Germany in 1904. It has a removable and interchangeable carriage. For a while the Torpedo was sold at export as the Regent.

The Weilwerke institution has grown into one of Germany's most important typewriter manufactories, the company pursuing a sound and aggressive policy and the machine standing high in the favor of the consuming public.

In 1914, the Weilwerke enterprise, in common with several other such procedures in Germany at the time, started to produce what was called the Torpedo-Simplex typewriter. This was a machine designed to cater to a clientele demanding a lower price in writing machines and appealing especially to the smaller user and tradesman. It is the same as the standard Torpedo except that a number of its features not required by that class of buyers have been omitted. Some of the features thus eliminated include interchangeable carriage construction, two-color ribbon, stencil cutter, etc., making possible a reduced selling price.

Travis

There is little available regarding this machine, though it was actually manufactured by the Travis Typewriter Company and we are at least able to say that it employed a ribbon.

Triumph

The younger of two writing machines of record named Triumph is made in Germany, it being a product of standard design with four banks of keys, single shift, and such other attachments

called for by the most exacting users as a decimal tabular, rapid escapement, etc.

The German-made Triumph typewriter appearing in 1910 as the successor to the Norica is one of Germany's better known standard machines of today. It has been very greatly improved and developed, the present model resembling the Underwood to no small extent. The Triumph is furnished with or without decimal tabulator and is made in six different carriage widths. The last model came out in 1921 in greatly refined manner.

Although originally made by the Deutsche-Triumph-Fahrradwerke A. G., bicycle manufacturers, the Triumph typewriter is now being manufactured and marketed by the Triumph-Werke of Nürnberg, Germany. In the earlier days of this machine's existence it was sold in France as the Mondiale and on various occasions in South America as the Edita, Phœnix and Koh-I-Noor.

Triumph (II)

To distinguish the Triumph typewriter of American conception we designate it as II, though it was an entirely different machine from the German product and had no connection with the latter. The Triumph Visible Typewriter Company, with its first offices in the Flat Iron Building in New York City, first announced their new $60 typewriter in March, 1907. It was made in a factory at Kenosha, Wis., from which city the report came in October.

1907, that a Receiver had been appointed. It was a short life that the Triumph Perfect Visible had.

The Type-Adder

No compilation of the many improvements and inventions leading to the typewriter's present high state of utility can be called complete without including the history of the Type-Adder which increases its usefulness to a high degree. In this field, this product is unique and deserves a place in this narrative.

For many years, special machines have been built wherein an adding mechanism and a typewriting mechanism are integral units, but each dependent upon the other for some common operating function. They cannot, however, always be considered in offices where the machine is also used for simple correspondence purposes. With this in mind, Julius C. Hochman and Maurice Samburg, both of New York City, set for themselves the problem of inventing a machine which would take the form of an attachment, applicable to standard typewriters. The present Type-Adder is the result of their work.

It is a complete and extremely compact adding and subtracting machine of a form developed for use in co-operation with typewriters of any standard make. Subtraction is direct, and not by the use of complementary figures. Attachment to the typewriter is a simple process. All typewriters have screw holes in their

frames adjacent to the keyboard, and the Type-Adder is provided with an attaching bar which fits the typewriter screw hole spacing. It is only necessary to remove the two typewriter screws selected, place the Type-Adder in position above the typewriter keyboard, and insert the longer screws in the same holes.

The inventors have also designed multiple totalizer attachments capable of adaption to systems requiring departmental segregation of costs or quantities, where individual totals of each column of figures would be required.

An examination of the accompanying illustration shows how cleverly the Type-Adder has been designed to conform to the space allowed by the typewriter, and by its neatness adds to the appearance of the typewriter. The two mechanisms work entirely independent of each other, but as combined they produce the effect of a single machine which adds and types simultaneously. Having its own carriage, the Type-Adder is independent of the typewriter platen and thus can perform computations either vertically or horizontally, with punctuation as desired, regardless of the position of the platen, which only controls the typed arrangement. The flexibility of such a combination is obvious.

The manifold uses of the Type-Adder include straight adding and listing, billing, statement writing, special report work, loose leaf accounting and the many other varieties of form work where combinations of typing and adding are required. It holds the unique position of being the only machine of its kind in the world. It is being manufactured and sold by the Type-Adder Corporation with offices in the Woolworth Building, New York City.

Unda

A short name for a small typewriter, the Unda is a ball-bearing, double shift, 31-key, front stroke machine weighing about 15 lbs. It also has a price of abbreviated amount. The Unda appeared first in 1921, although effort on it was commenced in 1913, interrupted first by the war and later by destruction of the factory through fire. This machine is manufactured by A. F. Bechmann,

G.m.b.H., of Vienna, Austria, and promises not unimportant participation in future history of the typewriter industry.

Uhlig

Another company was organized at Arlington, N. J., to make and market a typewriter invented by the same man, but the one here recorded was the Uhlig-Gunz Co., formed in 1910 for backing of a machine named after the inventor, Richard W. Uhlig.

Underwood

In relating to the compilers of this history his own experiences and the accomplishments of others in development of the great typewriter industry, the oldest living inventor of note, who has contributed of personal ingenuity practically no end of useful innovations and who long headed one of the most important typewriter manufacturing companies, in comment relative to placing of the type basket horizontally, made this gracious observation:

" . . . then the typewriter of today became evident and a greater visibility of writing ensued, so that this variation in the placement of parts became the settled form of today. The Underwood was the first to introduce this variation, but does not owe its popularity to this feature so much as to the introduction of the sublever for accelerating the typebar in making its imprint. This accelerating sublever was a real accomplishment in improving the typewriter. Similar levers were employed in other mechanical arts, but first in typewriters by the Underwood company. This device not only accelerated the typebar, but it rendered the start of the key in depression, light, and won favor immediately, and justly so."

While, as we indicate, the foregoing remarks were made in connection with comments on the subject of the present almost universal building of standard machines along lines in type baskets originated by the Underwood, the more interesting is what this old-time inventor totally without connection with the Under-

THE CONTINUOUS FANFOLD UNDERWOOD

wood enterprises says in further acknowledgment of merit in the Underwood typewriter. We would not be surprised in the least if those responsible for presentation of Underwood history in so far as it has to do with enumeration of mechanical features would be perfectly satisfied to have us stop right here. It is not often that one typewriter manufacturer openly pays such unselfish tribute to another, and even the most expert of Underwood inventors or most learned of typewriter historians could no better tell the story of the Underwood typewriter.

There has been a remarkable absence of change between the first machine made and the latest product of the Underwood Typewriter Company, i. e., as it refers to the regular correspondence machine and the writing mechanism of the various other Underwood products. The Franz X Wagner patent of April 27, 1893. was the start, the machine going through an experimental period by the Wagner Typewriter Company. The machine was bought by John T. Underwood, who had been associated with his father in the ribbon and carbon business of John Underwood & Company. He took as an associate, D. W. Bergen, still the treasurer of the different Underwood companies, and together they went through the initial struggle and have remained to this day in the same close contact.

The Underwood Typewriter Company was incorporated in

1895, in March, and offices were opened in the St. Paul Building, New York City, and a factory with floor space of 20 x 100 feet was taken on Hudson Street. The plant was moved in 1896 to Bayonne, N. J., where a four-story building was occupied. In 1899, the factory was again moved, this time to Hartford, Conn., where quarters three times as large were taken. The executive offices, which have always remained in New York City, were moved to 241 Broadway and growth compelled expansion in 1907 to all of the Broadway buildings at 241 and 243 and 3 Park Place as well.

The Underwood No. 5 is the correspondence machine of the Underwood company; hence, it is perhaps its most popular product. This model of the Underwood was placed on the market on June 28, 1900, since which time more than two million of them have been made. The typewriter is the medium through which the thoughts of business are expressed and by which the records of business are given permanency. The world-famous Underwood Standard typewriter is one of the machines that *"Speed the World's Business"* and give accuracy and dependability to writing and recording.

THE POPULAR No. 5 UNDERWOOD

The first departure of the Underwood company from sole supply of ordinary correspondence machines was in January, 1907, when the billing machine, the one for condensed charging, retail bill and charge and the unit bill and order typewriters were put on the market.

The Underwood Continuous Fanfold machine is a marvel of simplicity, and equally marvelous in results. After inserting the carbon sheets in the frame, the copies may be used until worn out without the necessity of reinserting them each time a bill is made, and the work is done with absolute accuracy, one of the principal features of all Underwood products.

If chronological order is observed, the next event of special significance was the reorganization of the Underwood Typewriter Company in March, 1910, by which it became a $14,000,000 corporation. The stock was listed the following month on the New York Stock Exchange. In August of the same year, Mr. Underwood bought the plot at 30 Vesey Street upon which the Underwood building was later erected. A factory addition which gave 50 per cent greater output through 163,000 sq. ft. more floor space was completed late in 1910.

THE UNDERWOOD BOOKKEEPING MACHINE

In January, 1911, the Underwood adding-typewriter first appeared, a part of the business which is really another story in itself. In May of that year another addition to the Hartford plant was of six stories and making a total of 575,000 sq. ft. The Underwood building at 30 Vesey Street, New York, was finished and occupied by the executive offices and those of all department heads in the same month that the big factory enlargement was put into service. The half-million mark in production of Underwood typewriters was reached on Monday, September 2, 1911.

It would be easy to go on with a paragraph for each year in relating Underwood history, but this is a condensed treatment and brevity must prevail at the expense of detail. The Underwood Bookkeeping Machine branch of the enterprise announced the "Addendagraph" in August, 1915, a separate company, John Underwood & Company, making and marketing these products. Until that time the adders had been made in the typewriter plant at Hartford, but during the year mentioned a new factory was occupied in Brooklyn. The year 1915 also marked a sorrowful event, S. T. Smith, long associated with Mr. Underwood, dying on May 4.

It is the policy of the Underwood Typewriter Company to supply the requirements and demands of its customers. This has resulted in the production of the Underwood Bookkeeping machine in response to the public demand for mechanical bookkeeping. This machine is so flexible that it may be adapted to any form of bookkeeping. Wherever used, the Underwood Bookkeeping machine has met with the greatest favor and by co-operating with its customers the company has supplied every feature that its increasing growth has suggested. Adaptability is the prime feature of this machine; as a result, it is a great time and labor saver.

Popularity of and demand for Underwoods to the exclusion of anything else reached what can be termed embarrassing proportions during the war. The machine was called for to such an extent by members of the army, navy and other government agencies engaged throughout America and allied nations in prosecution of essential activities as to leave the Underwood Typewriter Company in a position unable to supply anything like the customary number of ordinary commercial buyers of typewriters. As indicated, the war period developed a condition where popularity was a positive embarrassment.

In April, 1916, review of Underwood history shows the factory running nights to keep up with demand. Another big expansion in manufacturing facilities took place through start of material increase in May, 1916. The new service building at the corner of Vesey and Greenwich Streets in New York was announced in June of the same year. In December, George W. Campbell went to the Hartford plant for what developed later as superintendency of the making of another Underwood product.

By this time the members of the organization had begun to realize what the pioneers had gone through and what they had done in provision of pleasant employment and DeWitt C. Bergen, treasurer and close associate with Mr. Underwood since 1895, was made the recipient of a loving cup in recognition of his help in building up a great enterprise. This was in March, 1917, another event in the same year worthy of special mention being the opening in August of the new Underwood Service Building. A jump to November, 1919, and we note the appearance of the Underwood Portable typewriter, first made in the Hartford plant, but in May, 1921, moved to Plant No. 2 at Bridgeport, Conn., established for the exclusive manufacture therein of the latest of products to be added to the famous Underwood line.

The Underwood Standard Portable typewriter is still another answer to public demand for a typewriter that may be transported with ease. A portable typewriter, to be a success, must be light, strong and compact. All of these features the Underwood Portable has in the highest degree. It neither folds nor collapses. It is always ready for use when removed from the case

THE UNDERWOOD PORTABLE

without any adjusting. While it was intended especially for the traveling salesman, it has found so many uses that its possibilities are unlimited.

The sound proof cabinet is also a product of Plant No. 2 and was placed on sale in July, 1922.

The Underwood Soundproof Cabinet permits the use of the regular Underwood Standard typewriter—unchanged in any fea-

THE UNDERWOOD SOUNDPROOF CABINET (OPEN)

ture of its mechanical perfection, and takes up a few more inches space than the regular Underwood. Besides deadening sound, the Cabinet protects the machine from dirt, dust and accidental jars. It adds to the life of the machine and to its efficiency during use. The Underwood Soundproof Cabinet has behind it the experience, the technical skill and the resources of the largest typewriter manufacturer in the world.

More property was bought on Capital Avenue, at an estimated cost of $125,000, as recently as June of this year, for enlargement of the Hartford plant. The increase in capital stock of the company is too current to require reiteration here; the passing this year of the two-million mark in total of Underwood typewriters manufactured; these and many others could be enlarged upon if size of this special treatment required inflation.

The Underwood portion of this trade paper compilation in historical review of the typewriter industry would be incomplete without reference to the Underwood Computing Machine Company. Capitalized at $3,500,000 at the time of its organization in December, 1915, this company has since had full direction of the destinies from a manfuacturing angle of Underwood Bookkeeping machines. This company has its own plant at Hartford, Conn., in a building quite independent of the typewriter factory, and is officered by John T. Underwood as president, Emerson C. Eachel vice-president, D. W. Bergen treasurer and W. L. Dench secretary, the same since inception of the company.

Mr. Underwood and Mr. Bergen are also, respectively, president and treasurer of the Underwood Typewriter Company, Clinton L. Rossiter being the vice-president and J. E. Neahr the ranking department head as general sales manager. Charles D. Rice, factory manager, is the tower of strength who keeps things going smoothly and with ever increasing output at the big Hartford plant. Others; yes, many others, could, and perhaps should except for lack of space, be mentioned in connection with the development of the great enterprise headed by John T. Underwood, but this narrative must not be closed without saying that Frank M. Trevoe sold the first commercially manufactured typewriter in Washington, D. C., in 1874, and later introduced the typewriter for the first time in Europe when he went to England, where he has made his home these many years in like service to the Underwood throughout the Eastern Hemisphere. Still one more we wish especially to mention in this story—Horace W. Teele. Mr. Teele has been an Underwood man for forty-eight years, long before the beginning of the Underwood Typewriter Company, associated with the father of John T. Underwood in the ribbon and carbon business for many years and at present a director in the typewriter enterprise headed by the son of the original John Underwood.

Universal

The full name of a typewriter made in Germany and which was patterned much after the construction of the American Ben-

nington was the Universal Silbenschreibmaschinen. It possessed a sort of combination of type wheel and typebars and was devised for syllabic and word writing in ten languages.

Urania

Clemens Müller G.m.b.H., Dresden, Germany, besides making the Perkeo portable, also makes a standard machine of full commercially useful size called the Urania. It was first presented for

consideration of the distributing agents and buying public of the world in 1910, and is a visible writing, front stroke, four bank, single shift type of machine.

The house of Clemens Müller has been established since 1855 as sewing machine producers. Their typewriting machine, the Urania, has been greatly improved from time to time since its inception as a natural result of long manufacturing experience and enjoys today a good domestic and export sale. It is very favorably regarded in typewriter circles acquainted with it, embodying, as it does, most of the accepted principles of modern typewriter construction.

To the Urania correspondence machine, adding and subtracting totalizer mechanism was added in 1920, this machine being called the Urania-Vega. It was the first German typewriter to embody in its construction this very essential calculating feature.

The Urania was for a time before the war sold in France as the Gallia and in several of the Near East countries as the Ujlaki, named after the representative in that territory.

Vasanta

There are quite a number of instances of typewriters first introduced to the fraternity during the present year that are mentioned in this trade paper celebration of the fiftieth birthday of the writing machine industry. One of the several to enter the arena on the semi-centennial anniversary was the Vasanta typewriter, manufactured by Vasanta Aktiengesellschaft, Dresden 15, Germany. Only in the last number of this international organ of the trade a new model, known as No. IV, of the Vasanta was first announced. It is the same in many respects as the previously mentioned Meteor machine, though the Vasanta is greatly refined and improved and has been made to apply not only to demands for portability but for use in the heavier office work if occasion requires.

Velograph

A machine also using an indicator over its keyboard, the Velograph was the first typewriter to be made in Switzerland. It was invented by Adolph Prosper Egges, of Freibourg, and first sold in 1894, both in Switzerland and France. The Velograph was a slow writing machine, the keyboard being a semi-circular chart with a revolving indicator and the price low.

Victor (I)

Again it is necessary to distinguish between two machines of the same name. The Victor typewriter of 1894 invention was the devising of F. D. Taylor and F. A. White, of Hartford, Conn., and manufactured by the Tilton Manufacturing Company of Boston, Mass. This Victor, which we designate as (I), retailed at $15, made very little headway and was of the variously presented indicator type of machine upon which it was possible to write only with one hand while the other moved the pointer about.

Victor

Under this heading we present details of the Victor machine and business well known to the entire industry and a factor in the typewriter industry of active force. The United States patents of greatest importance covering features of the Victor Standard typewriter began with one issued in August, 1907, and there has been a continual succession of patents granted every year up to and including 1923. The Victor has always been pretty thor-

oughly covered by patents issued by countries foreign to the United States, this being particularly true with regard to the improvements on the current Model 10.

J. A. Hagerstrom was the principal inventor and engineer in connection with the development of the Victor, being assisted through the years by Geo. W. Campbell and others. The broad base, pivot-bearing typebar, which is an outstandingly chief feature of the Victor, is an invention credited to Wm. H. Hulse, who came from Montreal, Canada, and who was for a period several years ago actively connected with the Victor company. A typebar with two legs and its bearings an inch apart, whoever created it, stands out prominently as identifying part of the Victor's construction.

The machine was first developed in Boston, the Victor Typewriter Company as a New York corporation being organized in April, 1907, with offices and factory at 812-814 Greenwich St., New York City. This new company absorbed all interests of the old Franklin Typewriter Company, referred to elsewhere, discontinuing the Franklin typewriter and putting out the new machine which continues today in much like its original design with factory and general office now at Scranton, Pa. The foreign sales office remained at 338 Congress Street, Boston, until December 1, 1909, at which time it was merged with the other departments in New York.

There was a Model 1 and Model 2, No. 3 being put out to meet new requirements of the industry in February, 1912. Although later sold there under its own name, Model 1 Victor typewriter was originally sold, especially during 1908, in several European countries by its representatives there as the Dictator.

As will be recalled by those who follow events, ownership of the Victor enterprise passed into possession of the International Text Book Co. several years ago and it was shortly after that when a $2,625,000 corporation was formed to buy outright from them the entire assets of the Victor and operate as the Victor Typewriter Manufacturing Company. This did not materialize and the factory was moved in 1917 to Scranton, Pa., the home of the International Text Book Company in operation of their famous International Correspondence Schools. Mayne R. Denman was elected president of the Victor Typewriter Company on December 1, 1915, and he has continued to occupy that post

through the former and the present ownership now separate from I. C. S. interests. This severance took place in February, 1921, Everly M. Davis being the new financial head.

For the past six years the Victor Typewriter Company has made but little effort to develop trade in the United States, attention almost in its entirety being devoted to the shipment of machines to various foreign countries. The No. 10, which was put out in November, 1919, is the model towards which efforts of Mr. Denman and his associates are directed.

Victorieuse

A machine named Victorieuse is a child of the year 1893 and is described by reading what is said under the heading of the Gardner typewriter.

Virotyp

The Virotyp is a little pocket typewriter made in France by Machines à écrire "Virotyp," 30 rue de Richelieu, Paris. It is still being made and sold. It was in 1914 that it was announced ready for the market.

The manufacturers of the Virotyp have just put on the market a new apparatus which will have a great success through the manufacturers' world. With a very uncommon patented system, it will be possible to write with typographic types, on any design, counter-drawings, etc., at any inclination or position of the machine, and the writing will always be clear and visible. With the indelible ink used, reproduction on blue paper comes out perfectly.

After a short apprenticeship, the speed one can get is greater than handwriting. It is so simple that anybody can use it after a few minutes. Figures, letters or signs, with visible result,

THE NEW VIROTYP APPARATUS

can be printed on any point or line with exactitude. Every designer's office is a prospect for this ingenious and cheap apparatus, the price of which is 195 franc. Besides, the beauty and regularity of the writing recommend the Virotyp.

Visigraph

Mention of this machine constitutes a continuance of the story of typewriter inventions by Charles Spiro, previously mentioned in connection with the Columbia of early days and the Columbia Bar-Lock which made its initial bow as a pioneer in the typebar field in 1888.

In 1910 Mr. Spiro designed and first manufactured the Visigraph, a front-stroke model and possessing all Bar-Lock improvements. This machine enjoyed a large sale first by the Columbia Company previously mentioned and later by the Visigraph Type-

writer Company, which succeeded the former. In May, 1919, the factory of the Visigraph Typewriter Company at 37-41 West 116th Street, New York City, standing on a plot 100 x 100 feet, was sold and the building later altered for other purposes. At about the same time the company last mentioned was sold to the C. Spiro Manufacturing Company, 68-72 East 131st Street, New York City, of which company Mr. Spiro is president in association with his sons, W. J. and F. L. Spiro.

In July, 1919, the typewriter fraternity was pleased with the announcement of a new model Visigraph brought out by the C. Spiro Manufacturing Company. It had the modern knife blade typebar, rapid carriage escapement, universal bar operated by the typebars and many other features in recommendation of the name applied, New Visigraph Standard. That machine was later sold to the Federal Adding Machine Company and was renamed the Federal typewriter, under which heading can be seen another illustration of that latest product of Spiro invention.

Vittoria

This newest of Italian writing machines, appearing in the forepart of this year, is a standard single-shift, 88-character machine
of attractive design and thorough utility. It gives the appearance of good construction, has all the usually required standard features and promises to fill a place of importance in the typewriter world. The Vittoria is manufac-

tured by the large and long-established firm of S. I. M. S. Fratelli-Bertarelli of Milano, Italy, prominent manufacturers of precision machines. Effort was given to a writing machine starting after the close of the war and the Vittoria typewriter just put on the market is the outcome.

Volks

A low priced and simple machine manufactured by Fr. Rehmann, of Karlsruhe, Germany, in 1898 was called the Volks. With a chart for what in bar machines is called a keyboard and with

an indicator to locate the desired characters this machine had many brothers and sisters who were born and died during the period of typewriter manufacture which this issue commemorates.

Walker

What was claimed to be a noiseless typewriter was invented by C. Wellington Walker of Stamford, Conn., in 1910. He had been for 18 years with the Union Typewriter Company up to 1909, leaving to bring out what, in addition to noiselessness, was claimed to be a ribbonless, basketless, motionless carriage innovation in typewriter construction. Mr. Walker sold producing rights to Boston parties in February, 1912, but nothing further has been heard of the Walker typewriter.

Wallace

This machine, named after its inventor, was experimented with in New York for about five years commencing 1912. It was a portable typewriter of three rows of keys and double shift, seemingly of good construction and low in manufacturing cost. The inventor was a chemistry instructor in Columbia University and died several years ago; as a result nothing has been come of the machine.

Waverly

The typebars on this machine stood erect, but unlike other similar creations of its period, 1889. Instead of striking on a platen behind the bars, the carriage was situated between the keyboard and the typebars, so that the latter moved forward and downward, with resultant visibility. The Waverly had 40 keys, writing 80 characters and the printing was done from an ink roll. A later model, however, used a ribbon. This machine was sold chiefly in England, was invented by Edward Smith Higgins and Henry Charles Jenkins of London and was manufactured by the Waverly Typewriter Company, Limited, of the same city.

Wellington

Known as the Empire in Great Britain and Canada, the Wellington was the name under which this machine of long and popular existence was marketed in the United States. Its history is
much the same, therefore, as that by which the Empire typewriter is reviewed. An event which created no little interest among members of the trade in September, 1907, was the bringing on the market of a Wellington with standardized keyboard which made touch typewriting on it a reality. The election of C. W. Davis as president and

Alex. Dubé as general manager of the Williams Manufacturing Company, makers of the Wellington, in 1908, was also noted in printed references here reiterated. They are both to this day affiliated with the same company.

Westphalia

C. W. Brackelsberg of Hagen, Westphalia, who spent much of his life in typewriter effort, was the inventor in 1884 of a writing instrument named after the Province in which he lived. He also made an electric model, but the products of this inventor disappeared shortly after appearance on the market.

Wiedmer

The Schreibmaschinen Fabrik, H. Weidmer & Company, Bruchsal i. B., Germany, offered a small sized and light weight machine in 1907. H. Wiedmer was the inventor of this typebar machine which never reached the state of manufacture. A model was displayed in 1907 at the Berlin Exhibition of Office Necessities.

Williams

The invention of John Newton Williams, of Maine, in 1887, the Williams typewriter was one of the most popular machines its day produced. It was manufactured by the Williams Typewriter Company at Derby, Conn.

Entirely different in construction from anything hitherto produced but famous for its original visible writng, the Williams was a typewriter of high grade and entirely satisfactory usage. It had a three-row keyboard and wrote 84 characters in the machine covered by the first typewriter patent granted to Mr. Williams in 1875. With this a good degree of success was recorded, but the inventor would have profited and won more fame for himself had he been able to combine the necessary resources before 1892, in which year the machine was placed in manufacture in really substantial quantities.

The typebars on the Williams lay flat on the same horizontal plane as the platen, half in front and the other half behind the platen. In operation the bars struck with a kind of jump through an arc to the printing point on the platen. It was visible writing to a degree, paper previously written on except for the line immediately in process disappearing under the carriage. The latest product was a four-bank machine.

In May, 1909, W. S. Downs, a banker in Derby, was appointed receiver of the Williams Typewriter Company, though he continued to operate the plant by order of the court. In the meanwhile the 20-year charter had expired and there were other difficulties, including a restraining order involving patents, which mitigated against rejuvenation of the Williams enterprise. Transfer of ownership took place and a reorganization brought about the Secor Typewriter Company as the successor to the Williams Typewriter Company.

Woodstock

The Woodstock Typewriter Company was a change from the Roebuck Typewriter Company. After equipment for quantity production of the factory at Woodstock, Ill., the building and occupancy of which is mentioned elsewhere as the closing chapter of its predecessor, exhaustive research and experiment resulted in placing upon the market in September, 1914, almost at the time of the beginning of the World War, the No. 3 model Woodstock typewriter. The name Woodstock was adopted after the town of Woodstock, Ill., where it had its inception and is now manufactured. The machine was a complete success from the beginning and the company has never found it necessary to withdraw any of its models from the market, or at any time to call in machines for replacement or rebuilding because of defects or failures in design, material or construction. During the year of 1915 the No. 4 model was brought out, and its manufacture and sale increased constantly until it was finally discontinued in accordance with the war-time suggestion of the United States Government, asking for the elimination of all styles and models which could be dispensed with. At that time the executive offices now located in Chicago were housed in the factory at Woodstock.

In February, 1916, the capital stock of the company was increased from $250,000 to $600,000 and further expansion of manufacturing facilities and broadening of selling organization was started. About November 1, 1916, the No. 5 model was placed on the market. The current machine of this model embodies all the devices and features to be expected in a strictly high-grade

American typewriter, also a number of unique features exclusively controlled by the Woodstock Typewriter Company.

The No. 6 model, with 14½-inch carriage, was brought out about the first of the year 1922, and the No. 7 model, also a wide carriage machine, taking paper 18½ inches wide, was first offered for sale in the early part of 1923. The No. 6 and 7 models are, in general design, similar to the No. 5, but with the capacity for handling wider paper.

The export department of the Woodstock Company was organized at the beginning of the year 1917, at the same time that the No. 5 model was brought out. The sale of the machine in the foreign field has extended to every corner of the world, and the

THE LATEST WOODSTOCK PRODUCT

Woodstock is now looked upon in all countries of the world as "one of the well-known standard American typewriters." It is very doubtful if another typewriter has ever before invaded the markets of the entire world in so brief a period, and with such satisfactory results. Improvements and refinements are added from time to time as a result of inventive talent constantly employed to make of the Woodstock a typewriter worthy of the place in leading ranks which it is rapidly winning everywhere.

During the war and the expansion period following, only about one-tenth of the orders from the foreign fields could be filled, and the company were many thousand machines behind their orders. And in spite of present adverse business conditions abroad, exports have continued on the reputation which the machine had already established, and barring the first effects of the business depression Woodstock exports have shown a material growth.

WIDE CARRIAGE WOODSTOCKS ARE NOW BEING MADE IN VARIETY

At home the progress of the Woodstock has been no less striking. The Domestic Sales Department has built up an efficient organization covering the entire country operating through district managers and independent distributers. The sale of the machine through these channels has always been satisfactory and has shown a persistent and consistent increase. In the early part of 1922 the Branch Office Department was organized, and is now operating branches in fourteen cities of the United States, each in charge of an experienced manager with a full corps of salesmen and facilities for the best service to Woodstock users.

From the beginning it became known that the Woodstock was easy and convenient to use; that it had more speed than could ever be required in any business office; that it would turn out the very finest grade of typewritten work; and continued to do this for a remarkably long time. It was in conservative England that the Woodstock first began to gather in special honors for its performance in actual practice. At the Efficiency Exposition in Manchester, England, held May 31 to June 11, 1921, an operator who had never seen the Woodstock until he found it in the Exposition defeated the former champion for Great Britain in a half-hour contest by a margin of more than 30 per cent.

At the Business Exposition held in Paris in July, 1921, the French Championship for Speed was won on the Woodstock typewriter, and at the same exposition the Championship for Perfection of Work, which is of still greater importance to the typewriter world, was also won on the Woodstock. The judges of the contest took occasion to especially commend the work of the Woodstock for its superior excellence. At a contest held in connection with the same Exposition in Paris, October, 1922, both these championships were again won on the Woodstock. In a contest held in New York, in connection with the annual Business Appliance Exposition, the Woodstock typewriter was operated for a full hour at a gross speed of 121 words per minute, and the operator announced at the close of the contest that he could not charge the machine with a single error.

The Woodstock is the constant recipient of expressions of appreciative recognition, coming spontaneously and without solicitation. Recent advice through the State Department at Washington indicates that the Woodstock has been given a gold medal by the Jury of Awards at the Centennial Exposition held this year in Rio de Janeiro. Considering that of the short nine years since the advent of the Woodstock typewriter the first four were war years and the rest marked by abnormal and fluctuating business conditions it would seem to require no gift of prophecy in the light of past progress to predict a future of well merited success for the Woodstock typewriter.

The president of the Woodstock Typewriter Company is Dr. L. W. Meckstroth, the general sales manager is Vorley Wright, the export manager is Arthur Williams and the manager of branches is D. M. Alkire. Development of the Woodstock as a machine and growing importance of the company as a manufacturing enterprise is an outstanding successful addition to the typewriter industry during the last decade.

World

Another to be added to the long list of indicator type of machines is the World, made by the Typewriter Improvement Company of Boston, Mass., and on the market since 1886. It was invented by John Beeker, also of Boston. The alphabet in regular order from left to right on a semi-circular chart or disc which revolves tells the story of the World, a toy typewriter.

Xcel

In its proper alphabetical order under his name a syllabic writing machine invented by Wesley Henry Bennington is mentioned. Although the first was several years ago, another attempt by the same inventor to put out a machine of that character re-

ceived its initiation in April, 1922. Similar, but improved and refined, the new typewriter writing syllables and short words in addition to the usual alphabet in upper and lower case is called the Xcel. The Xcel Typewriter Corporation was formed by Mr. Bennington and general offices opened at 41 East 42nd Street, New York City, the Liggett Building.

Yetman

The Yetman Typewriter Transmitter Co., New York, was incorporated in July, 1907, with capital stock of $1,500,000. A factory was established at North Adams, Mass., and reported in full operation and machines being shipped in February, 1908. The Yetman machine was for telegraphic transmission of typewriting, one machine to another in distant point. The real property of the company was sold at auction on June 7, 1909, for $29,148 and J. L. Schmidt of Philadelphia bought the machinery and patent rights for $10,000.

Yost

This machine was given life in the plant of Merritt Brothers, Springfield, Mass., in January, 1887, the invention of George Washington Newton Yost. F. A. Young was employed in its building, the first being of the non-visible family and with a double keyboard. The ingenious construction of the typebars, by which they left their position of rest against an ink pad entirely surrounding the full circular frame or drum of the machine and travelled to and through a close fitting and alignment assuring guide to the printing point under the platen, has never ceased to this day to provoke astonishment to the uninitiated. Rightly, the original Yost typewriter was universally and early christened "the typewriter for beautiful work."

George Washington Newton Yost was an inventor and engineer who had been concerned in the production of earlier types of writing machines, and who had thereby gained practical experience of every typewriter invented up to that time. As a result of that experience, he laid down two essential features—(a) that the alignment of a writing machine could only be satisfactorily maintained at the printing point by means of a guide, and (b) that the ink must be supplied by an inking pad.

Naturally these features were embodied in the first Yost model ever sold, and it is a remarkable tribute to the genius of the inventor that during a period of progressive successes of over thirty-five years' duration, it has not been found possible to improve upon either of these first principles. The typescript produced on the Yost typewriter is claimed to be without equal amongst other machines, and, by reason of its direct-inking feature, it has been found particularly suitable for the preparation of lithographic transfers and for original work which is to be reproduced by the photo-offset process.

Shortly after the first Yost appeared on the market, it was found possible slightly to improve the escapement, and, this being accomplished, "The New Yost" made its debut. In 1895 the

BENNINGTON'S SYLLABIC

THE OLD AND THE NEW

No. 4 model of the Yost was placed upon the market, to be followed, towards the end of 1902, by the Yost No. 10. About this time the attention of the mechanical and constructional staff was directed towards the task of building a single-keyboard visible writing machine. Their efforts were highly successful and a few years afterwards the Yost No. 15 appeared, and was an instant success. This, in turn, was followed in 1912 by the "Improved No. 20 Yost," in which a high standard of typewriter efficiency was reached. In this model a number of improvements were made; the speed of the machine, always high, was placed beyond mechanical limitations; the typebar was rendered doubly effective and powerful in carbon and stencil duplication, and a new type of roller bearing was introduced into the carriage mechanism.

No insignificant factor in the success of the Yost has been the specialized provision made for the requirements of various businesses and professions. Chief amongst these are, perhaps, the quickly interchangeable carriages; commencing with the ordinary foolscap size, with a writing line capacity of 8½ inches, and made in various lengths, up to the largest known carriage (the No. 20F Yost) with a writing line capacity of 36 inches.

Yost machines can be supplied for writing in many languages, and special mention should be made of the achievement which produced a machine for writing in such languages as Turkish, Arabic and Persian. These languages, being written from right to left, contrary to the writing of the western world, necessitate a reverse movement of the carriage. Their numerals, however, being written in the same way as our figures (from left to right), render a carriage capable of being operated in both directions a necessity. Constructional difficulties were, however, overcome, and machines equipped with double-movement carriages and differential spacing mechanism were placed upon the market.

Early in 1914 a further important step was made, and The Yost Accounting Machine was produced. This machine, being fitted with adding and subtracting mechanism, is adapted practically to every kind of figure work, and when need arises, can be used as an ordinary typewriter for correspondence purposes.

The front-stroke visible writing Yost made its initial appearance in December, 1908, being a platen shift machine; this was called the Model "A" in the United States and Canada and No. 15 in overseas markets. The latest model of the Yost typewriter is a basket shift machine. While sold in a limited way by the American Writing Machine Co., the Yost typewriter has from its inception had its principle market in the Eastern Hemisphere. This characteristic, like its adherence to direct inking, is outstanding. The Yost machine, which was first introduced to the British public on the formation of the present company in 1891, is still broadly sold by the Yost Typewriter Company, Ltd., whose headquarters are in London.

Yu Ess

Named, as we interpret the intention, in letter spelling either of an abbreviation of "United States" or "Union Schreibmaschinen" the Yu Ess typewriter was introduced to America in April, 1918, by the Yu Ess Manufacturing Company of 200 Fifth Avenue, New York City. It represents an European patent and the same machine as the Mignon of Germany. In November, 1919, the general offices of the Yu Ess were moved to 511 West 42nd Street, shortly after which the undertaking ceased to operate. Visible writing and novel in construction, but of the indicator, one-hand type of machine which is naturally slow was the Yu Ess. Interested in the Yu Ess were John T. Cosman, for several years connected with the Mignon in Berlin, Lucius N. Littauer, head of the largest glove manufacturing enterprise in the United States, and W. P. Hatch, one of the inventors of the original Elliott-Hatch book typewriters and who, at the latest writing, was still trying to bring the Yu Ess under the name of Eclipse to a successful introduction in France.

An effort was also made to manufacture the Yu Ess in France under the name of Stella.

Zalsho

In alphabetical arrangement of paragraphed references comprising the greater part of this abbreviated history of the typewriter industry, there are other places where this machine might

be classified, for it was also called the Sholes, the Sholes Visible and the Z. G. Sholes typewriter. In fact, it was first heard of as the Acme, and is so referred to elsewhere, but as it appeared once with this distinctive designation we place it here under the heading of Zalsho. Moreover, by this placement a machine invented by a descendant of the original C. Latham Sholes who was responsible for the birth of the typewriter industry 50 years ago both starts and ends the paragraphed descriptions of this section.

Zalmon G. Sholes, son of C. Latham Sholes whose memory has gone down in history as the originator of the principle upon which the first commercially successful writing machine was based, was the inventor of the front-stroke, visible, four-bank machine

which identified him with typewriter history. Following the Acme fiasco at Waterbury, Conn., Mr. Sholes went to London and started the Zal G. Sholes Typewriter Company at 28, Victoria Street, Westminster, S. W. He succeeded in interesting what was termed the H. Lee Davis Syndicate, and in January, 1913, the Zalsho typewriter came out with identification of the Lawrence Manufacturing Company of London as the makers.

In July, 1915, the undertaking was discovered to have met serious interference because of the war and the product appeared again in America as the Z. G. Sholes typewriter at Wilmington, Del., where models of a machine with some improvements were being built in the plant of the Standard Arms Mfg. Co. The Typewriter Development Co., Du Pont building, Wilmington, was then in charge, and in November of the same year it was said that a newly formed Sholes Standard Typewriter Company would take over from the Typewriter Development Company all the assets and establish a plant at 511 Orange Street, in the same city. Executive offices were opened at 60 Wall Street, New York City, and Everly M. Davis was announced as the president of the new manufacturing company.

Zalmon G. Sholes died on October 9, 1917, and up to the present there has been no revival of his ambitions undertakings.

In Conclusion

As said introductorily, there is much more that could, with ample appropriateness, have been included in this portrayal of contributing factors in development of the great typewriter industry as it stands today. Up only until the time this trade paper was started in 1905, 2,678 patents on typewriting machines had been issued by the United States Patents Office alone. An analysis of the most important of those and mention only of thousands of patents granted since that time in all countries would fill volumes; dry reading to some perhaps, but nevertheless enlightening in their showing of thought given to the subject of mechanical writing. While many inventions found their way to adoption in some fabricated product, more were less useful or less fortunate in command of attention. All, we like to think, had some influence upon the industry—no less so because it is beyond possibility to include them in full tabulation in this necessarily abbreviated history.

Neither do we concede that the enterprises started but now non-existant were without benefit in planting the foundation upon which the structure of the industry has been built. Failures in common regard and ventures unprofitable to their sponsors have ofttimes shown the path to success for others. This would all be told in a complete history of the typewriter, which, permit us to acknowledge, wonderful as it is in its romantic aspects, this compilation does not purport to be. There have been practically no end of epochal inventions which deserve detailed description, hundreds of models have been put together by hand and remained unchristened, and little is known of others which actually had names. In the latter category are included some which many men now selling typewriters never heard of, such as the American Standard, Blind, Bonita, Buckner, Burnett, Burns, Competitor, Conde, Conover, Crary, Don, Edison for the Blind, "Eggis" Cypher, Gynee, Haughton, Hyndman, Herrington, Kent, King, McLaughlin, Menier, Mossberg, Oblique, Osborn, Pneumatic, Travis, Typograph, Union and Viktoria.

During the last fifty years the world has progressed more than it had hitherto done in thousands of years. This great progress is directly due to the discovery or development of means of communication such as the telephone, aeroplane, wireless, etc. The contribution of these to the world's progress has been considerable and the typewriter, the least spectacular, undoubtedly has

been more instrumental in the world's progress than anything else. To say that the typewriter has revolutionized commerce is no exaggeration. It requires little thought to realize that quick and efficient methods of communication are the dominant factors in present-day development and of all these, the typewriter is the keystone.

It is fifty years ago since the typewriter was raised from an interesting but obscure experiment to a commercial proposition and during that time it has become an indispensable adjunct to commerce. In its experimental stage there were many pioneers who invented weird and wonderful methods of writing mechanically, but with a few notable exceptions the present-day typewriter in general principle conforms to one that was designed by Sholes and put on the market half a century ago. In the early days, the typewriter, like all new things, met with a lot of opposition the chief of which was that a typewritten letter was too impersonal and that a client or customer who received one would lose faith in a firm sending it; they thought they were not receiving attention personally from the proprietor or partner of the firm in question. In the changing of this order of things alone the typewriter was of great service to commerce by breaking this old tradition that was limiting the scope of many, now colossal, business houses.

The typewriter is ever expanding its field of utility and though it has accomplished much in the last fifty years its future scope is great and the next fifty years will see an even greater development. It is a truly great industry that has developed since the first recorded invention in 1713 and the serious start fifty years ago to build typewriters for commercial use which this issue celebrates. No longer is the writing machine in competition with the pen, as it was when many of us first entered the business. It has monopolized commercial correspondence. Office work could not go on with expediency or commerce continued in volume without it. Bookkeeping will eventually be done entirely by machinery. The day will come when its utility in the home will be universally recognized. It will render obsolete the school room copybook for the child in learning his first lessons. Of such indispensable value is the typewriter.

The illustrating electros below of European machines were received at a date too late to place them in their descriptive classifications.

THE DACTYGAM, MADE IN FRANCE (*See Page* 27)

THE ITALIAN INVICTA TYPEWRITER (*See Page* 40)

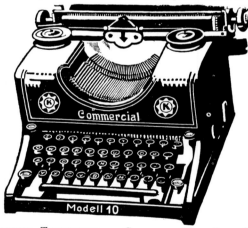

THE COMMERCIAL TYPEWRITER OF GERMANY (*See Page* 25)

THE EXCELSIOR TYPEWRITER (*See Page* 32)

Addenda

Developments in writing machine manufacture since the original printing of the foregoing and additional illustrations collected during the interim from October 1, 1923, to the publication date of this reprinted edition—August 1, 1924.

The Corona Four

The illustration herewith shows the new four-bank model officially released on May 1 by the Corona Typewriter Company, Groton, N. Y. It is appropriately designated as the Corona Four, having four banks of keys, in companionship with Model 3 with its three rows. The new model is non-folding, has a different typebar action, is fitted with a bail in replacement of paper fingers, has platen knobs on both ends, two extra feed rollers, automatic ribbon reverse, etc. The double shift machine will be continued at a retail price of $50 while the Corona Four is priced at $60 in the U. S. A.

Remington—Noiseless

In the January, 1924, number of "Topics" appeared the announcement of the amalgamation of the marketing facilities of the

Remington and Noiseless companies and the formation of the Remington-Noiseless Typewriter Corporation to continue the manufacture of the formerly named Noiseless machine at Middletown, Conn., for distribution thereafter by the organization of the Remington Typewriter Company. The same machine is now marketed throughout the world as the Remington-Noiseless typewriter. Dr. Charles W. Colby is chairman of the board and Benj. L. Winchell is president of the new corporation.

Picturing the Unda Typewriter of Austria

In its proper alphabetical order, mention is made in the body of the historical compilation first appearing in the October, 1923, number of "Topics" of the Unda typewriter manufactured by Maschinen & Metallwerke A. F. Bechmann, Ltd., in Vienna. We show herewith an illustration of the Unda typewriter, occupying a position midway between a portable and standard machine, which has now found a very satisfactory market both in offices and for private use. Further features not hitherto mentioned regarding

this recent addition to Austrian typewriter manufacture are the type guide which secures exact alignment, provision for a dead key, two-color ribbon and stencil cutting ability.

The Cardinal Typewriter

Our readers will be interested in the Cardinal typewriter, herewith illustrated, which is being manufactured and marketed by the famous watch works of L. Furtwängler Söhne, A-G, Furtwagen (Baden), Germany, an institution 100 years old and employing more than 600 workmen.

The Cardinal typewriter, a standard machine in every respect, embodies the four-bank keyboard, ballbearing typebars, thorough visibility, tabulator, back-spacer, and practically every other modern characteristic contributory to successful distribution.

The Mitex Typewriter

In the first edition of this History, there was no reference bearing the heading of Mitex, the name which appears on the typewriter here illustrated.

There is a statement, however, under the heading of "Tell" to the effect that a portable machine formerly known as the Mitex is now being manufactured by the Tell Schreibmaschinen G.m.b.H., Spandau-West, Germany. Since the initial printing, a block of the Mitex has been unearthed  and it is used in this Addenda as augmentation of the story about the typewriter now known as the Tell.

The Correspondent Typewriter

There was nothing said in the historical compilation as it first appeared about the Correspondent typewriter. To help make the Condensed History of the Writing Machine to that extent more complete, we show herewith an illustration of this little three-bank machine manufactured by D. N. V. "Acohama," Department of Office Machines, Keizersgracht 722, Amsterdam, Holland. The Correspondent typewriter is direct inking in its printing mechanism, instead of the more generally utilized ribbon.

Recently Appearing German Portable

A portable typewriter made at Frankfurt a. M., Germany, called the Diamant, is mentioned in the alphabetically arranged story, but without illustration. The latter is provided herewith —machine and carrying case.

The Swedish-Made Halda Typewriter

In further mention of the Halda typewriter briefly referred to in alphabetical order, it can be said that Halda Fickurfabrike AB. was founded in 1887 by Mr. Hammarlund for the manufacture of watches. A few years later experiments were started on a typewriter and the first of the finished product left the works in 1897. Several models were manufactured, the latest ones being the No. 9 and No. 10. During the years 1916-17 the factories were enlarged and the name altered from that mentioned above to AB. Halda Fabriker. The Halda manufactory employs 500 hands, has a steam kitchen supplying 300, barracks for 60 hands and 20 houses tenanting employees.

The New Dayton Portable Standard Typewriter

Herewith is an illustration of the machine made by the Dayton Portable Typewriter Co., 378 E. First St., Dayton, Ohio, mentioned briefly in the body of the History. It was put on the market in April, 1924, at a retail price of $35 in the U. S. A.

The thought back of the development of the "Dayton" was not so much to produce a light portable machine, as to bring out a simple and thoroughly durable typewriter that would do office work as well as home work, and still have sufficient lightness to enable the purchaser to carry it about without difficulty. The machine weighs 12½ pounds. The object was to produce a strong rugged typewriter that would stand up under heavy service.

The Dayton typewriter does not present features that are new and untried. The company's engineers have adhered to standard practice throughout, but through patent design they have eliminated a large number of parts by engineering study and simplification of mechanical movements. The average typewriter has 2,000 parts, and some of them have over 2,500. The Dayton, including every small screw and stud, has only 559 parts.

A New Phonetic Typewriter Invention

The Atlanta Model Machine Company, 1306 Candler Bldg., Atlanta, Ga., has been organized for the purpose of financing the 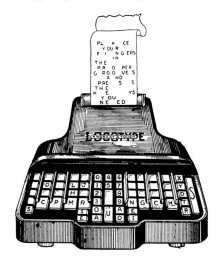 detailed designing and construction of one or more working models of the "Logotype," a combination writing and shorthand machine invented by Edna G. Robenson of the same city.

From the accompanying illustrations an idea can be gained of what this new machine is like. All of the consonants are on the left and right sides of the keyboard, some duplicated for the convenience of operations. Some keys are higher than others, similar to black keys on a piano, forming grooves in which the fingers remain and thereby simplifying fingering. The work is typed on a narrow strip of paper, words and syllables coming one after and under another.

To-days' Model of the Ideal

Like most of the historical compilations, the regular story about the Ideal typewriter leaves nothing to be desired in-so-far as

the narative goes, but the only illustration therewith was of the original machine first put on the market by these pioneer makers of writing machines in Germany. Therefore, we are making it a point to show in this Addendun a block of the present machine being turned out from the modern plant of Seidel & Naumann A-G. at Dresden.

A Better Picture of the Erika

It is not an especially good block which we used in the absence of anything better at the time in illustration of the Erika typewriter, manufactured by the old German house of Seidel & Naumann, so we reproduce herewith a later received line-cut of that little machine reposing in its handy carrying case.

The Vasanta Portable No. IV

The illustration herewith of the Vasanta typewriter supplements the paragraph in the main compilation as originally published and here reprinted in description of that recently appearing writing instrument.

The Wheel Printing Edelmann

Here is another illustration of a typewriter listed in its proper place in the History but with nothing to show exactly what the

machine looks like. Although made on the same principle, the Edelmann here pictured had a somewhat different arrangement of the indicating mechanism as compared with the first models.

Illustrating the Courier Typewriter

We said in the brief mention of the Courier typewriter, manufactured in Vienna, Austria, that it bore a very close resemblance to the American-made Oliver No. 3. The picture of the Courier which we are now able to make a part of the re-printed edition of the History of the Typewriter verifies the statement.

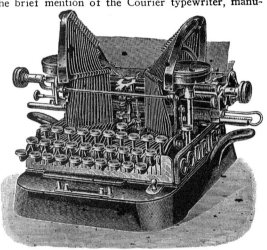

A New Standard Typewriter Made in England

In the February, 1924, number of "Topics" appeared the initial announcement of the new "British" typewriter now being marketed by the Blick Typewriter Co., Ltd., 9 and 10, Cheapside, London, E. C. The company named, headed by Mr. Geo. G. Rimington, took over the interests of the former Salter Typewriter Company and entered into an agreement with Messrs. Geo. Salter & Co., Ltd., West Bromwich, England, manufacturers of the Salter typewriter, to built this new front stroke standard typewriter.

The first model was completed in April, 1923, from designs worked out by Salter engineers in conjunction with Mr. Rimington. It is a full-sized machine, writing 88 characters, possesses some special features, combines tested and tried principles and in workmanship and materials is of high grade British manufacture. The "British," which is marketed in Great Britain as the "British Blick," will be sold in all countries of the world as the product of a combination of manufacturing and merchandising experience dating back over thirty years.

The Standard Mercedes Typewriter

In the body of the History the machine illustrated in conjunction with reference to the Mercedes typewriter is the electrically driven model; herewith we show the regular correspondence machine, which is the same as the presently supplied Electric Mercedes except it is without the motor attachment. The first Electric Mercedes was also the first practical electrically operated typewriter. The manufacturers of the Mercedes now occupy their own building at Berlin-Charlottenburg 2, Berlinerstr. 153, and the firm was recently converted into a Joint-Stock Company. A brisk business is carried on in England by the Mercedes Typewriter Co., Ltd., whose managing director is Mr. Hendrik Jansen, a well-known and successful man of affairs.

A distinction claimed by the manufacturers of the Mercedes typewriter is that it is the "grandmother" of all other more or less demountable typewriters. Even the first model was made in three separate units—frame, carriage and type-basket. Confidence engendered through intimate knowledge of all working parts, ability to readily keep mechanism clean and utmost ease of operation have contributed to the success of the well-proportioned Mercedes typewriter. The present standard machine is Model 4, exactly like Model 3, except for the in-built tabulator supplied in all ordinary deliveries.

Illustrating the Saxonia

The name and address of the supplier, Franz Lippmann, Mulheim-Ruhr, Germany, was given in the brief paragraph which

listed the Saxonia typewriter in the first printing of this Condensed History of the Writing Machine. Herewith is a half-tone reproduction of that machine.

A Chinese Typewriter Sells at $240.00

With the exception of the rubber roller and the ribbons, a machine originally invented by Shu Chen Tung, an engineer of the same concern, the whole mechanism of a Chinese typewriter is made by the Commercial Press Works of China. The roller works in the same way as ordinary typewriters, but it can be moved in all directions over the surface of a square tray containing more than two thousand characters grouped according to roots.

Picturing the Heroine

A very interesting story about Franz Heumann and his Heroine typewriter appears in its proper place in the regular treatment, but at the time the first edition went to press we had no illustration of the machine which could be used in connection herewith. In supply of the earlier deficiency, the accompanying picture is made a part of this Addendum.

Made in the Bing Works

There is no illustration in the regular classification and description of the Orga typewriter, the supplying of which here is occa-

sioned by the re-printing of the original text and this Addenda. A recently issued catalogue calls special attention to the inbuilt billing device, long carriages, tabulator, etc., as features not enumerated in the earlier compiled description.

Underwood Typewriter With Quiet Appliance

There has been placed upon the market by the Underwood Typewriter Company, a quiet appliance which fits around the sides and back of

the machine, designed to meet the needs of quietness in business offices. No feature of construction in the typewriter is impaired, the appliance being almost unnoticeable and adding, if anything, to the attractiveness of the machine in appearance. The quiet appliance is sold for a very nominal amount.

Relative to the Fitch and Williams Typewriters

Alexander G. Hug, in comments from his place of business at 128 N. La Salle St., Chicago, clears up some points of history about the old Fitch and Williams typewriters. Mr. Hug substantiates his personal knowledge through the fact that in 1887 he was selling the automatic check punch patented by E. N. Williams
(Continued on Page 107)

Reg. U. S. Pat. Off.

**The only
Computing Attachment
for Typewriters**

For fifty years the typewriter has been only a correspondence machine.

Now, with the aid of the TYPE-ADDER it can also do—

*Adding
Subtracting
Billing
Statement Writing
Loose Leaf Bookkeeping
Special Report Writing
Form work of all kinds*

The work is completed in the one operation of typing. Totals are computed by the TYPE-ADDER simultaneously with the typing. No extra operations are necessary. No special forms are required.

**At last
A Billing Machine
within Everyone's Reach**

Any standard typewriter will do this with our TYPE-ADDER attached. No special training is required—any typist can operate it.

The TYPE-ADDER can be attached in less than 3 minutes. It does not interfere with the normal use of the typewriter.

Price **$60**

*No Typewriter is Complete
Without the TYPE-ADDER*

TYPE-ADDER CORPORATION

Woolworth Building   -   -   -   New York City

Cable Address: "Typeadder" N.Y.

WHAT is the future of the typewriter industry? What is the goal? Surely it is that the typewriter shall become the universal writing instrument used by every man, woman and child. And this means that the big work ahead will be centred around the "portable" and therefore "personal" typewriter. It is a wonderful future and a great opportunity.

CORONA TYPEWRITER CO., Inc., GROTON, N.Y.

The Personal Writing Machine

"PORTABLE!"

The Word that Revolutionized Writing and the History of the Typewriter Business

From a commercial point of view, what are the two most important things that ever happened in the typewriter business?

Obviously the first was the introduction of the practical typewriter in September, 1873. Typewriter history started then, and for the next thirty-three years the business grew steadily, as machines were made more efficient and public interest increased.

Then came 1906—the year when a typewriter was designed which did exactly the same work as an ordinary machine, but which was light enough and compact enough to be carried anywhere. The first Corona had arrived.

Yet why was that event so very important? Because at a stroke it multiplied the size of the typewriter market ten times—fifty times—nobody yet knows how much. Previously every business house had been a possible purchaser. After 1906 *everybody* became a prospect.

Such tremendous possibilities were not realized at the time. The Corona portable typewriter (at that time called the Standard Folding) had to fight against all kinds of obstacles. It won out and its history from then until today is well known throughout the industry.

Corona led the way in 1906. It leads today. Over half a million people have proved that Corona is designed and built *right*. No other typewriter has been so thoroughly tested. Used and abused by all kinds and classes of people under every possible condition it has never failed to stand up and prove its worth.

So that today Corona has a worldwide reputation for durability and dependability and *there are more Coronas being used than all other makes of portable typewriters put together.*

The new CORONA FOUR with standard four bank keyboard

*I*N silence, in swiftness, in sturdiness, the L. C. Smith Typewriter is unexcelled.   No other writing mechanism interposes fewer mechanical obstacles between the thought of the executive and its expression in type.

Ball bearings at every important frictional point; uncanny lightness of touch; perfect writing vision; right or left-hand carriage; greater silence---these are a few of the features that make the L. C. Smith Typewriter excel in point of daily quantity as well as quality of work.

Write for an interesting booklet, "The Greyhound of the Office," which explains.

L. C. Smith & Bros. Typewriter Company

Factory and Executive Offices—Syracuse, N. Y.

Branches in all principal cities

Sole Dealers for British Isles:
L. C. SMITH & BROS. TYPEWRITER CO., Ltd., 19, Queen Victoria St., London, E.C.

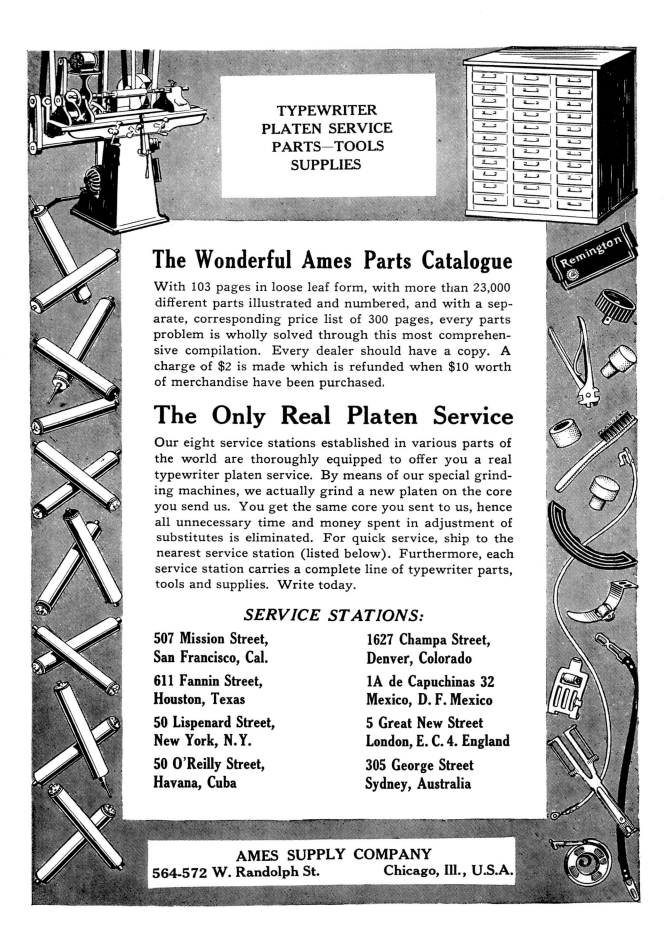

BRITISH
and
BEST

The BRITISH an 88 Character High Grade STANDARD
TYPEWRITER of entirely BRITISH manufacture

THE PRODUCT OF MANY YEARS' EXPERIENCE IN MANUFACTURING COMBINED WITH MANY YEARS' EXPERIENCE OF WHAT IS WANTED IN A TYPEWRITER

GOOD AGENTS WANTED IN ALL COUNTRIES

THE BLICK TYPEWRITER CO., Ltd.
9 & 10, CHEAPSIDE   **LONDON, E. C. 2**

Important Dates in Typewriter History

1873   THE FIRST TYPEWRITER
1893   SMITH PREMIER TYPEWRITER
1923   NEW SMITH PREMIER No. 60

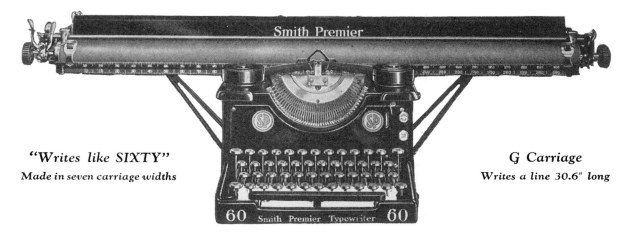

"Writes like SIXTY"
Made in seven carriage widths

G Carriage
Writes a line 30.6" long

It is fitting that the semi-centennial year of the invention of a practical typewriter should produce a new model, THE SMITH PREMIER No. 60.

Thirty years ago the old double-keyboard Smith Premier was considered a marvelous piece of office equipment. And rightly so. The typewriter itself was then only twenty years old and the Smith Premier represented a big step forward.

The new No. 60 Smith Premier, the achievement of steady progress brings together speed and fatigue-reducing qualities in a lighter, more compact typewriter.

Ten important improvements built into the Smith Premier 60:

1. *Open face construction.*
2. *Light, rigid, vibrationless carriage.*
3. *Extra-size platen.*
4. *Simple positive ribbon mechanism.*
5. *Four position ribbon adjustment.*
6. *Type bar segment shifts.*
7. *Type bars completely controlled.*
8. *Convenient margin release and tabulator keys.*
9. *46 keys print 92 characters.*
10. *Cushion-like touch.*

SMITH PREMIER
TYPEWRITER CO.
376 Broadway   New York, N. Y.

50th Anniversary
of the Typewriter

1873

Model 1 Remington. The first practical typewriter and the ancestor of all the writing machines in the world today

Cut from the first typewriter catalogue (1874). This picture of the girl at the typewriter was prophetic of the millions of women who have since earned their living through the writing machine

Christopher Latham Sholes, inventor of the typewriter, at work on one of his experimental machines (1872)

FIFTY YEARS AGO, in September, 1873, at the Remington Works, Ilion, N. Y., began the manufacture of a new machine which was destined to revolutionize business, free the world from pen slavery, and complete the economic emancipation of womankind. No other machine, no other invention, no other article of commerce of any kind has ever played a more commanding role in the shaping of business and social destiny.

Christopher Latham Sholes was the inventor of this machine, Ilion, N. Y., was its birthplace, and Philo Remington was its first manufacturer. Originally known simply as "The Type-writer," it is now known to fame and history as the Remington Model 1.

We are proud of our record as the founders of this great industry. We are equally proud of our many contributions to typewriter development, which have been continuous throughout the entire fifty years of typewriter history.

The first shift-key typewriter, writing both capitals and small letters (1878), was a Remington.

The first typewriter equipped with an automatic ribbon reverse (1896), was a Remington.

The first typewriter equipped with a decimal tabulator (1898) was a Remington.

The first adding and subtracting typewriter appeared in 1907. It was a Remington.

The Remington brought out the first automatic line indenting mechanism (1908), the first key-set decimal tabulator (1911), the complete accounting machine (1914), and the first portable typewriter with complete, four-row standard keyboard (1920).

Here is a record of progressive pioneering unparalleled in the typewriter industry —but even this does not complete the Remington story.

The latest and greatest Remington contribution to typewriter progress is the new Quiet 12. This new Remington is quiet in its operation. The "natural touch" makes its use a pleasure to the operator. The completely enclosed frame is a protection against dust and dirt, and helps to keep the machine in good working condition. And refinements in the printing mechanism insure good work—always.

This latest Remington is a fitting product of the comprehensive and unrivaled experience of its builders. It has the sum of every quality any user has ever wanted in a writing machine.

1923

Model 12 Remington The culmination of 50 years of typewriter progress

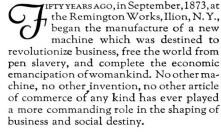

Remington Typewriter Company
374 Broadway, New York ❧ **Branches Everywhere**

The standard folding Hammond retains every feature of the desk-type machine yet weighs only about 8½ pounds.

The NEW
Hammond Typewriter

VARIABLE SPACING—CHANGEABLE TYPES

The only totally DIFFERENT Typewriter Offered the Public in the last 30 years

Its great variety of uses places the New Hammond typewriter beyond comparison with any other machine.

The Hammond principle of construction is *different*.

Its work is also *different,* and the possibilities for its use in new fields of mechanical writing are practically unlimited.

The New Hammond is the only variable spacing typewriter and in addition has these exclusive features:

TWO STYLES OF TYPE OR TWO LANGUAGES always in the machine and changed at the turn of a knob.

INTERCHANGEABLE TYPE SHUTTLES, placing at the disposal of every Hammond owner 17 different styles and sizes of type and special characters for more than 50 languages.

AUTOMATIC TOUCH assuring uniform impression of each character—like a printing press—whether the key is touched lightly or pressed heavily.

THE VARIABLE SPACING gives uniform spacing between letters for all the different sizes of type; 10, 15, or 18 characters to the inch, instantly changed by touching a lever.

AN INTERNATIONAL TYPEWRITER

Every Hammond writes in over 50 languages. There are two different type styles or languages always in the machine, and others can be instantly substituted.

Write for complete description, prices, and agency terms. The Hammond is known in every civilized country. Its universal adaptability makes this the best sales opportunity ever offered.

HAMMOND TYPEWRITER CORP., 500 East 133rd Street, New York, U.S.A.

The **AEG** Typewriter

The AEG, in addition to possessing all the features of a modern writing machine, has some special patented improvements. All machines are supplied complete with tabulator and automatic device for letter spacing.

> The AEG Typewriter is rapidly gaining a world-wide reputation, such as is enjoyed by our other products.

Agents wanted where not represented.

A E G – Deutsche Werke

Schreibmaschinen Gesellschaft m. b. H.

Export Department

BERLIN W 66, Germany

The Dayton Standard Typewriter
that's portable

THE $35.00 Dayton (in the U. S. A.) will open up for the Typewriter new markets of great extent that have never been touched.

Our modern system of intensified quantity production—with only one size and one style—makes this possible. We use the same methods in production and sale of the "Dayton" as Henry Ford does in making his car.

Then too, we have eliminated literally hundreds of parts, as our PATENTED DESIGN requires only 559 parts, as compared with over 2,000 parts in other standard machines.

The Dayton weighs only 12½ pounds, but all parts are of a size and strength equalled only by a few of the large, heavy types.

It has the full Standard 4-bank keyboard—two color ribbon—spacing lever—marginal release—two shift keys, and shift lock.

It easily produces six clear, perfectly legible copies—has exceptional speed—and its visibility is unequalled, being at the natural reading angle.

The typist will not have any new habits to form in operating a speedy, Standard Dayton.

MADE ONLY BY

The DAYTON Portable Typewriter Company

378 EAST FIRST STREET   **DAYTON, OHIO, U. S A.**

Cable Address { *"Daytype Dayton"*
Western Union Code 5th Edition }

Today's standard

IN design and construction the Royal Typewriter from the very beginning took shape as the ideal writing machine, a machine which would do the best work, the fastest work, and do it most easily at the least expense.

These ideals have found a practical solution only through constant application and ceaseless effort over a long period of years—not by one individual, but by hundreds of men with the same object in view—a better built typewriter.

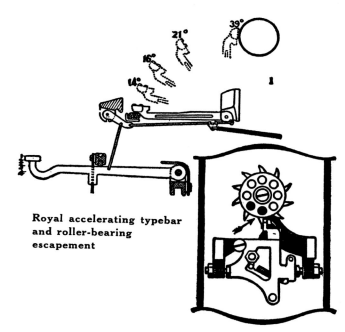

Royal accelerating typebar and roller-bearing escapement

ROYAL TYPEWRITER COMPANY, Inc.
316 Broadway, New York   Tel. Worth 1400
Branches and Agencies the World Over

The DEMOS
CALCULATING MACHINE
Invented & Manufactured in Switzerland.

Some of the Features of the Demos Calculator

Same standard of workmanship as made Swiss watches famous the world over.

Simple and rugged construction.

Noiseless—Easy running.

Exceptionally rapid and reliable.

Easy to master.

No specially trained operators necessary.

Capacity—9 x 8 x 14.

Compact (12 x 6 inches desk space).

Portable—Light weight (14 lbs.).

The operator sees at a glance proof of the correctness of his multiplication or division.

Figures reset to Zero with one turn of the crank.

Fully guaranteed.

The new principle of Demos design fully patented in all principal countries enables it to be manufactured and sold at a price heretofore unheard of for a high class calculator.

Exceptionally favorable proposition for energetic dealers

H. B. COLES
46 West 24th Street, New York
Distributor for North America
including Mexico and Cuba.
Cable address: "Forcomser," New York.

THEO. MUGGLI
93, Bahnhofstrasse, Zurich, Switzerland
Manufacturer.
Cable address: "Visible," Zurich

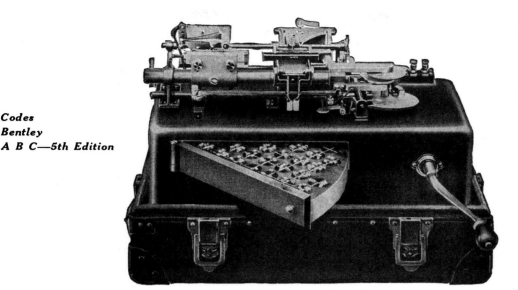

Codes
Bentley
A B C—5th Edition

Cable Address
Engragraph
New York

The Achievement of Engravograph

What the linotype has done for printing, the typewriter for letter writing, the adding and calculating machine for accounting is paralleled by Engravograph—the automatic engraving machine.

Engravograph is the mechanical perfection of a 4000 year old art.

Engravograph is so simplified in operation that after a few minutes instruction a child can engrave initials, names and addresses on a variety of items in a far superior manner than can be accomplished by the experienced hand engraver. Engravograph completes a line of engraved character in *three minutes.*

To the progressive retailer Engravograph offers a complete engraving service at a fraction of the cost to him of hand engraving.

Engravograph attracts customers who come in to the retailer's store to have personal items engraved and to purchase other items which can be so identified.

Complete information about Engravograph available upon request

The Engravograph Corporation
90 West Street, New York City, U. S. A.

Forty-four Years of Faithful Service

THE SEAL OF QUALITY
AND SERVICE

FOR forty-four of the fifty years since the typewriter first came into existence, we have been manufacturing or rebuilding typewriters until today the American Writing Machine Company is the oldest concern of its kind. Year by year we have kept up with the progress and development of the typewriter, and have kept faith with the trade by rigidly maintaining our policy of *Service* and *Quality*.

OUR FACTORY TODAY COMPLETELY OCCUPIES THIS LARGE BUILDING—EVERY DEPARTMENT UNDER ONE ROOF.

FACTORY IN 1910

"INVINCIBLE" Rebuilts have set a standard. They are noted for their durability, workmanship and finish. Our stocks include an assortment of Fixed-up and Rough Remingtons and Remington Monarchs at prices which allow you liberal profits. Shipments from nearest of our conveniently located branch stores. Send for price lists.

RUBBER COVERS

For all makes of typewriters, adding machines, check protectors, multigraphing, addressing and folding machines and other office devices.

Your Name Printed Free of Charge
On Orders for One Hundred

This is a valuable form of advertising which you can get at small expense.

AWMCo Mechanics' Apron is another of our products. Dust, oil, cyanide and chemical proof, it protects the clothing. Manufactured from automobile top material. Neat in appearance. Requires no laundering, easily cleaned with soap and water.

TYPEWRITER SUPPLIES

"INVINCIBLE" supplies never fail to give complete satisfaction. They measure up to the high quality of all "INVINCIBLE" products. Included is everything for the typewriter—Ribbons, Carbon Paper, Transfers, Sizing, Oil, Enamel, Brushes, Pads, etc

Stock a trial order and see for yourself how well they will please your customers. Send for price list and let us know your requirements.

"INVINCIBLE"
TYPEWRITER SUPPORT

A big seller because it is so convenient and useful. Serves as an extra desk and takes up very little room. Easily attached to desk, table, wall, filing cabinet—anywhere. Can be used for typewriter, adding machine, index files, books, stenographer taking dictation, etc. Revolving top, etc. Revolving top (15x20 inches). Oak or mahogany finish. Strong black japanned support. Sells on sight. Liberal profits. Order a few or send for circular.

Retail Price
$5

Denver and West, $6.

PLATENS Re-covered

24 Hour Service From Our Conveniently Located Branch Stores

You save Time, Money and Transportation by sending your platens to be re-covered to the nearest of our conveniently located branch stores. We use only the best grade of rubber for this work. Specially constructed grinders operated by long experienced workmen, insure accurate work, absolutely true diameter and a perfect surface free from ridges and blemishes.

Send us your next lot of typewriter, adding machine or multigraph rollers to be re-covered. Satisfaction guaranteed.

Resident Salesmen Wanted

American Writing Machine Company

Branch Stores in Principal Cities
Home Office and Factory: 449-455 Central Avenue, Newark, New Jersey

The Relation of the Ribbon Spool to the Typewriter Business

Two outstanding fundamental improvements in the typewriter since its inception are—

> First   —*Visible writing.*
> Second—*The removable or interchangeable ribbon spool.*

Our purpose in this article is to consider only the second of these—the ribbon spool and its relation to the typewriter business. The typewriter inventor and his mechanical engineers have in almost every instance designed the ribbon spool as a part of a writing machine. He has been followed by the designer of adding and calculating machines, time clocks and recorders. The most important function of the ribbon spool has received little or no consideration; namely, a container or package, if you will, to carry and preserve the essential inked ribbon so that it may be quickly and cheaply delivered to the user.

No attempt has ever been made at standardization of the ribbon spool and the time does not seem ripe as yet, but second thought will certainly convince you that the ribbon spool is akin to the tire of an automobile, or a spool of thread for a sewing machine. After having once enjoyed the convenience of thorough standardization in automobile tires, you can readily picture the confusion that would arise and the increased cost of tires that would immediately follow the introduction of a plan whereby each model and each different automobile required a different size and make of tire. This exact situation is to-day causing the users of your machine to pay an additional and unnecessary tax on their ribbon supplies. If you will, put the matter the other way around; assuming that present prices are satisfactory to your consumers, the expenses of your supply department are just this much higher than they might be. It may

seem incredible that there are many typewriters and other office machines on the market who have gone to the trouble and expense of building their machine with a removable spool for which the only supplies that can be purchased locally or in the open market are stock ribbons wound on carrier spools which the operator has to rewind.

As to its effect upon the sale of the typewriter itself, simply consider this fact. Whether the ribbon spool costs two cents, ten cents, or twenty-five cents apiece, it is not a matter of serious import as a part of a hundred dollar machine, but whether the spool costs twenty-four cents a dozen, a dollar and twenty cents a dozen, or three dollars a dozen, makes just the difference between making a knocker or a booster of the supply man who sells the ribbons to your customer. Do not fool yourselves for one minute. The supply man who is in constant contact with the typewriter and other office machine users has unconsciously a tremendous effect on the purchaser of a new machine.

We are writing this article because we have been called upon from time to time by one after the other of the principal typewriter and adding machine manufacturers to work with them in simplifying and standardizing the ribbon spool so that it may compete with others on the market both as to price and availability.

The service costs you nothing whether it is of benefit to you or not, but there is one thing we can do, furnish you with a dependable supply and distribution of ribbon spools without initial cost for tools with which you cannot possibly compete either as to price or as to distribution as we are immediately able to put these in the hands of every ribbon manufacturer in the civilized world.

A Variety Line Brings More Sales

1 + 1 = 2 + 1 = 3

"We all know *that*" you will say. BUT—did you ever stop to think that

TYPEWRITERS
ADDING-CALCULATING MACHINES
CHECK PROTECTORS

will treble your sales possibilities? Sell your customers, COMING and GOING. He may not need a typewriter today, but *darn it,* he might have use for a check protector.

If he already has a checkwriter, there may be every reason why he ought to and should have an adding machine of some kind.

A reputation built on the fact that you can supply EVERY NEED in office machines will bring your customers to you every time and will attract many new customers.

At "lowest prices ever quoted" we are wholesaling and exporting on an unprecedented scale. Our volume is the secret of our prices and we are keeping every customer, because of quality and mainten-  ance of promises. Our price list and literature should always be before you. We carry in stock ALWAYS the largest variety and greatest number of machines in the country.

RELIABLE TYPEWRITER & ADDING MACHINE CORP.
Cable Address : Reliable 170 WEST WASHINGTON STREET, CHICAGO, ILL.

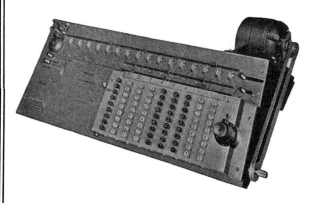

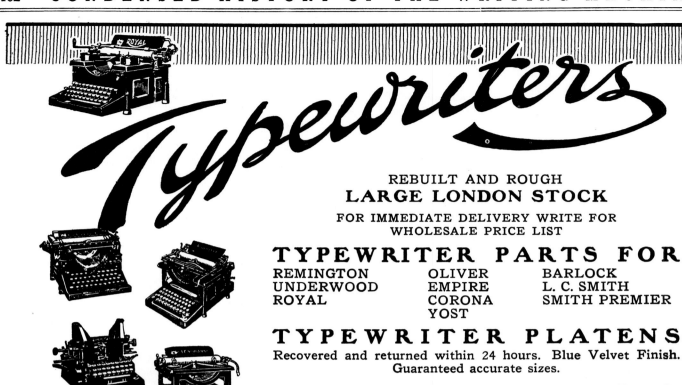

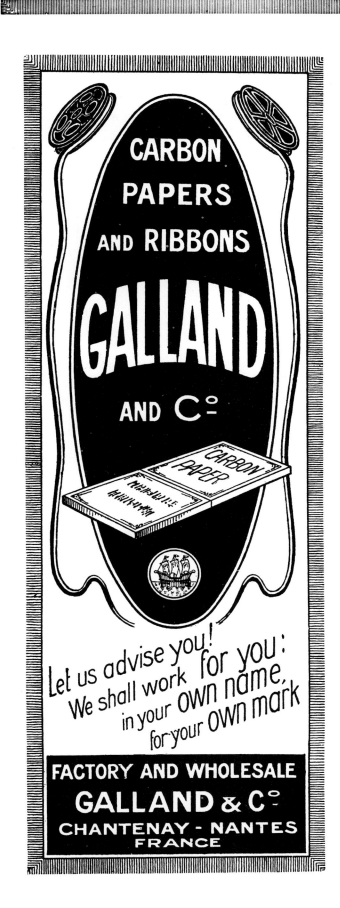

Fitch and Williams Typewriters

(*Concluded from Page 78*)

and made for Williams Brothers by the Brady Manufacturing Company of Brooklyn, N. Y. He continues:

"In 1888 Mr. Fitch brought his machine to the Brady Mfg. Co., where they were later made, and at that time E. N. Williams was building the first model of the Williams machine at this same factory. The Fitch machine was put on the market in 1891. Humphrey and Hinkley had the agency for it in Chicago and as I had the agency for the Williams check punch here I consolidated with them and also sold Fitch machines.

"In 1892 Mr. Williams sent on the first Williams machine to us at Chicago, and it embodied quite a number of parts of the Fitch machine (which by this time was found to be a failure). In 1892 we started a selling campaign and placed the machine on exhibition at the World's Fair and it was at this time that Mr. Andrews became president. Early in the year 1892 a contract was entered into between the Williams Typewriter Co. and the Domestic Sewing Machine Co. whereby the latter company were to manufacture and sell the Williams machine in this country, but in the summer of that year the Domestic Sewing Machine Co. went into the hands of a receiver and the Williams Co. bought back all their tools and started in at Derby, Conn.

"By strange coincidence, just after I dictated the above I met a Mr. Chase of the Chase Sign Co., Chicago, to whom I sold my first Williams typewriter in 1891; he informs me that he still has the same machine."

Adding to History of the Commercial Visible

Reference is made here to the compilation appearing on page 47 as first printed and the same material on page 25 of this reprinted edition of the History of the Writing Machine about the Commercial Visible typewriter. We are glad to add to and correct what was originally prepared through quotation from comments on the subject by Alex. M. Fiske, who wrote as follows under London date line:

"The illustration shown in your October number is not the Commercial Visible, but is the machine which preceded it under the same patents and was built to the number of, maybe, two or three hundred. The typewriter you picture was known as the Fountain typewriter and was built for and sold only to Siegel Cooper & Company. About two years later, in 1900, William Baldwin, who had acquired the patents from Uhlig, abandoned the idea of building that machine, having an entirely new model made; new drawings, patents, dies, jigs, etc., representing the later developments of that machine. A company was then formed called the Visible Typewriter Company, not the Commercial Visible Typewriter Company as stated. They proceeded to open a factory and produce machines which came out in 1901 under the name of Commercial Visible. It was at that time, during the making of the drawings and manufacture of the machine, that I became connected with the company. About three thousand typewriters were made and sold. The actual number of parts in the Commercial Visible exceeded 600."

Recent German Arrivals

The "Imperator" is a new typewriter first mentioned in the June, 1924, number of "Topics"; it is manufactured by Hegeling-A. G. Eitorf/Sieg (Rheinland), Germany.

An entirely new portable writing machine has just been put upon the market by Fritz Danziger, Berlin N. W. 21, Germany; it is called the "Gunda" and is being sold for 30-55 Goldmark.

Another new German product of the small variety, announced, like the foregoing, for the first time in July, 1924, "Topics," is the "Geka" typewriter, offered by Fritz Knipping, Braunschweig, N. O., Germany.

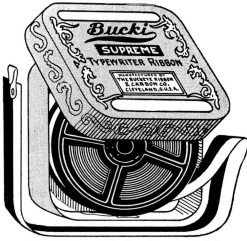

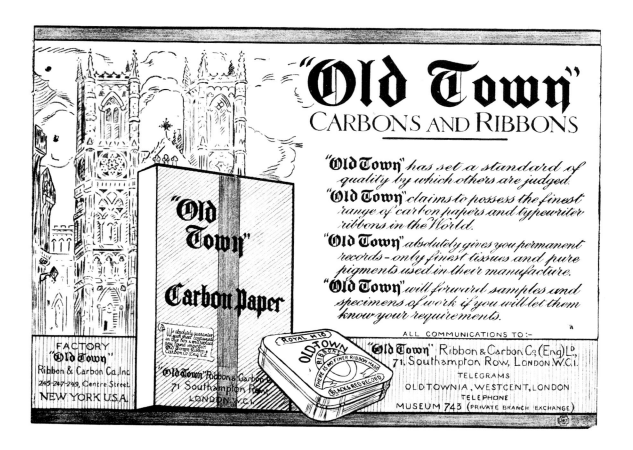

Fifty years ago
The typewriter ushered in the present order of office efficiency

With the increased communication that typewriter correspondence made possible, came the need for more systematic business records. Business had adopted a faster schedule. Vital facts must be at hand for IMMEDIATE reference.

Rand VISIBLE Records answer that demand. This VISIBLE system displaces old methods as thoroughly and as completely as typewriter displaced long-hand letters.

Every record of business is INSTANTLY available where Rand VISIBLE Records have been adopted. It is remarkable that the largest and most progressive companies in the country are using them?

Let us tell you how you can make money selling Rand VISIBLE Records and Rand VISIBLE supplies.

RAND COMPANY, Inc.   999 Rand Building
North Tonawanda, N. Y.

Originators and largest makers of VISIBLE card records.

Let us send you samples and prices. Your customers will want them as soon as they learn how much more serviceable price-books, directories, letter files, etc., can be made with these light, strong, durable, inexpensive indexes. Miles and miles of them are being sold to big concerns like the Bethlehem Steel Co., General Motors Corp., Marshall Field & Co., and others.

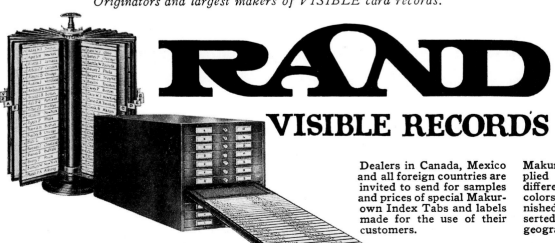

RAND
VISIBLE RECORDS

Dealers in Canada, Mexico and all foreign countries are invited to send for samples and prices of special Makurown Index Tabs and labels made for the use of their customers.

Makurown Index Tabs are supplied in six-inch strips, in four different widths and six different colors. Tabs can also be furnished ready cut with labels inserted in alphabetical, numerical, geographical and monthly sets.

All Embracing and Progressive to the Last Degree

¶ Every trade paper demand of the office equipment industry is met by the periodicals which we publish and every requirement in assistance to dealers in selection of merchandise to handle is supplied by the facilities of our Service Department—this includes every article used in a business office and the personal attention of staffs in our own offices on both hemispheres.

¶ The founder of "TOPICS" was among the pioneers in promotion of world-wide sales and was the first man in the world to project a trade paper for the office appliance industry, and in exercise of leadership ever since in all that has transpired in publishing development dominates the field in creative endeavor and constructive innovations—experience in the trade dating from 1894 and progressive application of all that is gained through aggressive management and many years of growth with the industry is bound up in the value of "TOPICS" as a news and service medium. Although imitated, it is without parallel anywhere in trade paper annals.

¶ Only through consistent reading of the monthly issues of "TOPICS" can any member of the great office equipment industry keep posted on all that takes place within the ranks of the trade in all countries of the world. Also, its subscribers have Free access to the benefits of the International Service Bureau, which, through intimate contact with what manufacturers are doing everywhere, is always able to arrange profitable agencies for worthy distributors. There is actually no need for office equipment men to read any other periodical —"TOPICS" gives all of the news, of all countries, and at a *very* low price: $3 for 2 years, if remitted to New York, or 12 shillings in British currency for 2-year subscriptions sent to our London office. To those who request it, we will also mail BUSINESS EQUIPMENT without extra charge, and under certain conditions a copy of "The History of the Typewriter" will be included as a premium to new subscribers; ask about this!

TYPEWRITER TOPICS

THE INTERNATIONAL OFFICE EQUIPMENT MAGAZINE

A special 2-year subscription offer is available

BUSINESS EQUIPMENT

The American Domestic Pictorial Trade Newspaper

Send for a sample copy

INTERNATIONAL SERVICE BUREAU

The Direct Link Between Buyer and Seller

Free to "TOPICS" subscribers

THE TYPEWRITER HISTORY AND ENCYCLO-PEDIA

Pictures the Ancient and the Modern
Portrays the Romance and the Realities

---

50 cents or 2 shillings per copy

Business Equipment Publishing Company

230 Broadway, New York, or Guildhall Annexe, 23, King Street, London, E.C.2

Taking the Ledger out of the Shadow of the Pen

OLD figures are treacherous figures. Last week's accounting is a matter of record—not an index of today's condition.

Books kept on the Underwood Bookkeeping Machine are rarely more than a day, often less than an *hour*, behind the last transaction.

Ledgers, for instance, are kept in *perpetual balance*. A trial balance can be struck almost automatically whenever desired. Statements are ready for mailing on the last day of the month —without overtime.

Think of the advantages in collections, credits, purchases, sales, in *all* branches of the business, that result from Underwood accounting—accounting that is taken "out of the Shadow of the Pen".

Executives will be interested in "Taking Industry Out of the Shadow of the Pen". A copy will be sent on request. Write to

UNDERWOOD TYPEWRITER CO., INC., Underwood Building, New York
Branches in all principal cities

CALL in an Underwood Bookkeeping Machine representative. Let him, without obligation, give expert advice on any accounting problem.

UNDERWOOD
Bookkeeping MACHINE

COLUMBIA Offers *the* World *of* Business
Only that which is *Right* in Carbons and Ribbons

WITH A THOUGHT FOR TOMORROW—when a *Better* sheet of Carbon paper can be created—or when a *Better* Typewriter Ribbon can be decided upon . . . . *Columbia* will make it!—and be proud to pass its product on as another step forward in business progress.

WITH THE FACTS OF TO-DAY—*Columbia's* Ribbons and Carbons are second to none for completeness—enjoy a world-wide distribution —and have the acknowledged reputation of living up to the letter of a guarantee "Satisfaction or No Sale."

A modern plant in New York, with impressive branches everywhere, assures the *freshness* of its product to the dealer and consumer alike.

A skilled staff of chemists and shopmen assures the Quality that America's business world regards as *incomparable!*

A specially organized Sales Division assures dealer service—coöperation—and better business relations. The dealers that now comprise the Columbia circle find it a profitable fact.

Are you interested in making your carbon and ribbon department a successful factor in the profits of your business? . . . . if so Columbia can build the foundation.

At the Service of the British Isles

Our London Factories are admirably equipped to supply direct! "Classic" Ribbons—the Best British Brand . . . and "Rattlesnake"—Highest Grade British Carbon are but two of the many grades instantly available.

COLUMBIA
Ribbon & Carbon Co., Ltd.
22 Bush Lane,
Upper Thames St.
London E. C. 4

At the Service of Continental Europe

An exceptional Continental Service, complete in every detail and ready to demonstrate Columbia qualities at any time. You are invited to put it to a test. All lines . . . in every grade.

COLUMBIA
Ribbon & Carbon Co., Inc.
Via San Sovino 1
Milan 32

COLUMBIA RIBBON & CARBON MFG. CO., Inc.
Home Offices and Manufacturing Plant
69-71 WOOSTER STREET, NEW YORK
Branches throughout the United States and Abroad

CHICAGO	MILWAUKEE	DETROIT
KANSAS CITY	PHILADELPHIA	MINNEAPOLIS
LONDON		MILAN

With the dawn of every business day more than 2,000,000
UNDERWOOD
typewriters go into action
Speeding the World's Business

UNDERWOOD TYPEWRITER CO. INC., UNDERWOOD B'LD'G. N.Y. *Branches in all Principal Cities.*